AF543144

RESTAURANT MANAGEMENT

Encyclopaedia of Hotel, Tourism and Hospitality Management in 21st Century Series

RESTAURANT MANAGEMENT

Edited by

Amrik Singh Sudan

ANMOL PUBLICATIONS PVT. LTD.

NEW DELHI - 110 002 (INDIA)

ANMOL PUBLICATIONS PVT. LTD.
Regd. Office: 4360/4, Ansari Road, Daryaganj,
New Delhi-110002 (India)
Tel.: 23278000, 23261597, 23286875, 23255577
Fax: 91-11-23280289
Email: anmolpub@gmail.com
Visit us at: www.anmolpublications.com

Branch Office: No. 1015, Ist Main Road, BSK IIIrd Stage
IIIrd Phase, IIIrd Block, Bangalore-560 085 (India)
Tel.: 080-41723429 • Fax: 080-26723604
Email: anmolpublicationsbangalore@gmail.com

Restaurant Management

© Reserved

First Published, 2002

Reprint, 2005, 2010

ISBN 81-261-1065-1

[Responsibility for the facts stated, opinions expressed, conclusions reached and plagiarism, if any, in this volume is entirely that of the Editor. The Publishers bear no responsibility for them, whatsoever.]

PRINTED IN INDIA

Printed at Mehra Offset Press, Delhi.

Contents

Preface

Hotel industry has close relation with tourism industry. With the flourishing of international tourism, Hotel industry has also gone drastic changes and has grown leaps and bound. In the current age of globalisation and liberalisation it is growing rapidly—having cosmopolitan touch. In true sense, hotel, hospitality and catering are enthusing the feeling of international integration, thus the world as a global village.

The present work is intended to bring together authentic information on diverse aspects of hotel, hospitality, and catering management such as—hotel management, restaurant management, housekeeping management, hospitality marketing, food and beverage management, and foodservice operations. The entire information is logically organised under above titles. The concepts and developments are supported by facts and figures.

To make the work comprehensive we have gathered the information from various sources. We are grateful to all the scholars whose writings are cited or substantially made use of in the present venture. I am also thankful to my colleagues and friends who have assisted me in one way or other while preparing the manuscript. Last but not the least, I am indebted to Mr. J.L. Kumar, Managing Director, Anmol Publications Pvt. Ltd., New Delhi for his constant moral support and also for bringing out this work within a short span of time.

—Editor

1

Introduction

Restaurant operational styles are of three major types: quick serve, family style, and full service. Within these three categories are restaurants which offer a wide variety of service styles from self-service to French service. Buffet, take out, and banquet service are some of the variations. All of these categories of operational styles are operated as both independent and franchise businesses. To be better able to understand the development and current status of these restaurant operations as businesses it is important to understand the difference between an independently owned restaurant operation and a franchise restaurant operation.

Independent ownership

Independent ownership may be by an individual or a chain. Both individual and chain restaurants can be operated by a single independent owner. The distinction between individual and chain is the intentional duplication of a restaurant operation into more than one unit. Many successful restaurateurs have taken a proven restaurant and found locations which will successfully support a duplicate of that operation.

Early restaurant entrepreneurs such as Howard Johnson and Bill Marriott provide excellent examples of the successful application of this practice. Howard Johnson found a highway intersection location to be highly successful. When major interstate roads replaced the original two-lane highways, his company moved quickly to provide roadside restaurants where customers had always found them, along major travel routes.

Independent restaurant operations are freestanding units. These operations may be owned and managed by individual owners or groups of investors.

Owners may be involved in more than one operation and often borrow successful ideas and incorporate them into another restaurant, depending on the theme, cuisine, and location. Some owners choose to put all of their energies into one restaurant.

The Hilltop Steak House in Saugus, Massachusetts, has consistently been one of the highest-volume single-unit operations in the United States. Averaging over $8 million annually, this restaurant seats 1100 and serves a limited menu which concentrates on high-quality beef dishes. Customers have been traditionally standing in line for a quality of food and service that they know will be consistent with their expectations.

Independent restaurant operations are financially based on the resources of owners and/or investors who expect a percentage of any profits made as a return on their investment.

Chains

Corporate giants have found that takeovers of smaller corporations have often yielded a chain of restaurants. Depending on the primary objective of the corporation, the chain may be sold off or absorbed into the company. Food-related companies such as General Mills have developed their own restaurant chains and kept them under corporate ownership rather than turning them into franchises.

Franchise

> Franchising is a method of doing business whereby a parent company (the franchisor) grants (via a franchise agreement) an individual outlet owner (the franchisee) the right to market its products and services while using the parent's proven name, reputation and marketing techniques.

Restaurant franchises are duplications of successful restaurant operations which are sold to individual owners or investors. An owner may have more than one franchise. Companies that sell franchises may also continue to own and operate some units for the parent company. These are called company-owned units and are not classified as franchises.

Financial arrangements generally include an initial franchise fee and require a cash investment by the investors. The parent company also receives a royalty on the earnings of each franchise. The amounts of fees and percentages of royalties range widely from one company to another, depending on each company's history of success.

Restaurant operational styles

Quick serve

Quick serve is the 1990s food service industry term for what has traditionally been called fast food. In the 1960s and 1970s the development of the fast-food restaurant chains, McDonald's, Hardee's, and Burger King, specializing in a variety of hamburger items and french fries initiated a wave of self-service restaurant chains that included Taco Bell, Kentucky Fried Chicken, Long John Silver's, and a host of others representing speciality foods and cuisines. These operations follow the basic format of providing limited seating in a casual atmosphere for customers who order at a self-service counter to "eat in or take out." In the 1970s drive-through windows were added to many of these operations, allowing customers to order over an intercom system located in the parking lot and drive up to a pick-up window for their orders.

The growth of this segment of the industry was in direct relation to the growth of the population group represented by the "baby boomers," or post-World War II birth group. Today this group is about to become the senior citizen population of the United States and still represents the largest and most important consumer group in America. As the baby boomers began their families, the demand for inexpensive food served quickly in a casual atmosphere suited, for families with young children reacted very favourably to the fast-food restaurant style.

In the 1980s this same customer group now began to look for more variety in fast food menu offerings as well as healthier items and methods of preparation. Fast-food restaurants responded in part by producing salad bars and prepackaged salad items.

In 1990 McDonald's Corporation was the largest purchaser of iceberg lettuce in the United States, according to the California Iceberg Lettuce Association, clearly showing the favourable reaction of the general public to these menu offerings.

The McLean Deluxe hamburger, developed in cooperation with the National Beef Council, represents a major attempt by McDonald's Corporation to present food items in response to the needs of their customers. Chains such as Wendy's introduced a self-service buffet bar offering Mexican and Italian cuisine items as well as salads. Pizza Hut developed a line of pasta dishes to augment their traditional pizza/sandwich menu.

Breakfast became an addition to many of the speciality hamburger and fried chicken chains in an attempt to recover slipping customer counts. By the end of the 1980s the increase in two-income families dramatically changed the life-style of the American family, creating an increasing demand for foods to take out to eat in. The take-out window was, in many operations, doing as much volume as the walk-up counter. In Sharon, Pennsylvania, the

Quaker State and Lube Restaurant does close to $1 million of business annually in orders of chicken wings from their one drive-up window Fast-food restaurants were beginning to turn into casual family-style restaurants on their menu boards but remained self-service in their operations. As the industry began to recognize the impact of the development of the take-out segment of their operations and other trends, adjustments were made to the marketing plans of a number of restaurant chains:

1. Quick-serve was developed to define casual family-style dining which could represent fast-food, fast-food/ family-style service combinations, or family-style service alone.
2. Take-out became a stand-alone restaurant concept.
3. Menu items that could be pre-prepared in a fast-food kitchen setting that also responded to the demand for healthy eating concerns were identified.

Pizza Hut Corporation has created a line of Carry-Out units which sell and deliver pizza as well as a selection of menu items from the red roof Pizza Hut restaurant menus. No customer seating is provided and drive-through windows are generally available. The company expects to have 3000 of these units located across the United States by 1995. In addition, Pizza Hut pizza will be made available to food service vendors in all segments of the industry from airlines to sports stadiums. This addition to their marketing strategy now allows the traditional Pizza Hut restaurant to concentrate on casual family-style service in a quick service setting with the fast-food line shifted to the Pizza Hut Carry-Out unit.

Family style

Family-style restaurant operations are represented by food service operations offering booth and/or table service in a casual setting. A combination of buffet and table service can provide labour-cost-reducing opportunities while giving customers variety in visual presentation as well as menu offerings. Independent as well as chain and franchise restaurants incorporate this service style into their overall operations.

National chains such as Big Boy's and Howard Johnson's are examples of family-style operations. Theme and cuisine restaurants such as Chili's, the Ground Round, and Bennigan's are blends of family-style/ casual dining. Family-style dining restaurants can offer alcoholic beverages but in the majority of cases do not.

Operations that offer breakfast/lunch services are often operated as independent restaurants whose owners work as chef/managers. Delicatessens with table service, cafeteria-style steak houses, and coffee shops are also examples of the variety of family-style operations.

Full service

Full-service restaurant operations are designated as those restaurants offering sit-down table service. A full-service restaurant is not defined by its price but by the type of service, atmosphere, and menu selection offered to the customer. Menus in full-service restaurants generally offer a variety of course selections from appetizers to dessert and include alcoholic beverages. Pricing of menu items can range from mid/low to expensive, depending on the theme, cuisine, and location of the restaurant. Full-service restaurants are generally independently or chain owned. The Chart House is an excellent example of a chain-operated full-service restaurant. The company operated sixty-two units nationwide in 1989. These restaurants often confine themselves to dinner service only with location as a primary feature. They are located on a waterway whenever possible to emphasize the water navigation chart theme expressed in their signage, name, and menu cover. The atmosphere is casually up-scale, and the menu offers a full course selection of regionally specialized items.

In Philadelphia, Pennsylvania, the Chart House is located on the Delaware River adjacent to the city. The architecture of the restaurant devotes all of the window space to water views. The lower level is a lounge and raw shellfish bar with dining on the upper level. Operation begins at 4:30 p.m. and caters to an after work and social clientele. The average check without alcohol is $15.

The economic recession of the early 1990s is affecting this segment of the restaurant industry more than any other. Full-service restaurants which flourished during the 1980s saw as much as a 50 to 60 percent decline in their customer counts in 1990 and 1991. Michael Hurst, former president of the National Restaurant Association, noted that the roots of this severe down-trend lie in major changes in the dining out preferences of the baby boomers who represented a large percentage of the previous customer base for this restaurant style.

Mr. Hurst noted, "Through the 1980's, this influential market segment sustained an interest in chic, experimental, high-priced dining establishments, but a variety of factors-aging, family building, a loss of confidence due to the 1987 stock market crash-has created another revolution in taste within this group. Today, baby boomers are looking for less elaborate meals in homelike surroundings and at lower prices."

The result of this change in customer needs and demands is a dining style called casual style. Full-service restaurants are adjusting their decors to reflect a less formal, comfortable atmosphere.

Menu offerings are being revised to include simpler food items with less labour-intensive preparation. American regional foods prepared by "home-style cooking" methods are returning to full-service restaurant menus in place of highly developed food ingredient combinations and plate presentations. This change in menu offerings has also allowed the menu pricing structure to be lowered to attract customers who are feeling the constraints on both business and personal spending for entertainment.

Healthier menu offerings include a wide variety of fresh seasonal greens and vegetables. Poultry has become the most popular low-cholesterol source of protein. Turkey and chicken are appearing in both traditional and experimental forms on restaurant menus.

Cooking methods also reflect healthy dining concerns as stir-fry, steaming, and grilling take precedence over deep-fat frying, roasting, and use of heavy sauces.

Healthy dining programs for full-service restaurants are the result of the combined efforts of local hospitals and area restaurant associations around the United States. Restaurant menus indicate items which have been planned under the supervision of hospital dietitians to respond to a variety of dietary concerns, including low-cholesterol and low-sodium cooking.

Restaurants provide nutritional breakdowns of the menu items for customers. This awareness of healthy dining concerns among restaurant customers responds to the basic needs of both middle-aged and senior citizen customer groups. The baby boomer senior citizen groups will be healthier, wealthier, and longer lived than ever before in the history of the United States. This consumer group will have a major impact on the food service industry for the next 20 years and will require its needs and demands recognized through programs such as these. All phases of the industry will recognize the necessity of incorporating marketing techniques which will encourage the attendance of senior citizen customers.

Concept dining

In the 1980s the increased costs of entertainment combined with rising menu prices created a concept called the destination restaurant. Operators realized that customers were, for economic reasons, being forced to choose whether to go out for either dinner or entertainment rather than combining both in one evening.

As a result, restaurants which offered both a dining and an entertainment package began appearing in a wide variety of themes and concepts. The Air Transport Command is one of a number of theme restaurants currently operated by Speciality Restaurants of Anaheim, California.

The restaurant combines a casual-style, full-service restaurant with an entertainment lounge. In addition, the World War II theme of the restaurant incorporates a location adjacent to the runway at a small airport which allows diners to watch airport traffic. Nineteen forties music and memorabilia combined with interior design features complete a package which provides entertainment for families as well as couples over an extended dining time period.

Developing a restaurant's destination possibilities can significantly increase overall business. There are, however, management and marketing considerations that must be evaluated. As managers and owners look to new ideas and concepts to increase their customer counts and profits, it is important to assess the needs of both customers and the local community creating a concept for which there is no demand will have disappointing results.

The initial phase of developing a market survey requires a knowledge of the statistics that make up the four areas of a market survey:

1. Community
2. Customer
3. Competition
4. Labour pool

It is necessary to research the demographic statistics of the community in order to obtain this information.

Demographics is the statistical study of the population of a community with reference to its size, density, population distribution, and vital statistics. This information is available in town and city halls and has been compiled from the national census that is conducted in the United States every 10 years. Additional updated information is sometimes available from the Chamber of Commerce and the local libraries. The information most helpful to owners and managers of food service operations for developing effective surveys and customer profiles is

1. Population
2. Sizes of age groups
3. Average family sizes

4. Breakdown of income averages within the general population
5. Major trends in growth and development in the community

The general economic health of the community is a major factor in the future success of a restaurant business. Communities forecasting a healthy continuance of businesses which employ significant numbers of the population will offer a steady restaurant customer base.

Communities suffering from difficulties in retaining or attracting businesses offer uncertainties in employment opportunities for prospective customers and an unsteady customer base. It is important to understand the profile of the business community in your area. The type of products and/or services provided by these businesses can often determine the forecasted stability of the business community.

In the United States, 75 percent of all businesses produce and/or provide services to the general population. Only 25 percent of businesses in the United States produce manufactured goods. Labour strikes, shortages of raw materials and energy supplies, and major changes in the demands for manufactured goods can close plants within weeks. An example of the effects of the closing of major sources of employment is provided by the statistics which accompanied the announcement of the closing of some military bases.

Total loss of jobs: 6158

Loss of military jobs: 1958

Loss of civilian jobs: 2700

Loss of related contract jobs: 1500

Total loss of income to community

Annual wage tax revenue: $1,000,000

Total loss impact on retail sales, real estate, and supporting services annually: $750,000,000

Employment income becomes revenue in the community dispersed on both necessary and disposable services and goods from food and clothing to apphances and automobiles. job loss and income reduction also affect the stability of the housing market and dramatically influences the overall economic health of the community.

Full-service restaurant businesses are often among the first to feel the effects of reduced customer spending.

Quick-serve restaurants generally thrive in this type of economic crimate when customers need to be able to purchase prepared food outside the home but can compromise on the style of restaurant they patronize.

Events that can affect a restaurant's success often occur outside the local community. Energy supplies for the United States are subject to international events such as the Persian Gulf War in 1990. This event threatened to reduce the flow of imported oil into the United States sharply. This reduction would have affected every major business area from transportation to food production.

During the 6-month period of this international conflict, restaurant businesses suffered severe cutbacks in customer counts. In addition, future food sources and supplies were questionable and prices fluctuated in reaction to this uncertainty. This was coupled with a national economic recession that had been affecting the country for an extended period before the Persian Gulf conflict.

Many restaurant operators were unable to sustain their businesses under the strain of both major national events and were forced to sell out or declare bankruptcy Those who survived this period recognized the necessity of applying basic business management principles to their operations, directing their efforts toward providing their target markets with the products and services that were most needed to retain customers.

Labour

The availability of qualified labour is one of the major problems facing restaurant managers in the 1990s. The demographics of the United States indicates a population whose largest group is represented by the baby boomers. The age group 24 years old and under, which traditionally provides the majority of food service employees, is the smallest population group. The result of this reversal of population group size is a dramatic decrease in the available labour pool for the majority of food service operations.

As a result, managers will have to expand into nontraditional labour pools to recruit the balance of their employees. This labour search will be concentrated on the senior citizen population, who are healthier and are expected to have a longer life span than ever before.

Training programs for both of these labour source groups are necessary to produce a qualified labour pool. The food service industry has been and will continue to be one of the strongest growth industries in the United States. Changing family patterns are continuing to increase the opportunities for growth in food service businesses.

Communities that provide job-training opportunities for these businesses offer managers a labour pool that has the asset of being knowledgable about their jobs and the benefit of training in a variety of food service job-related skills. Competition for these employees is forcing restaurants to increase their pay scales and offer benefit packages.

Job sharing and other adjustments in work schedules provide more employment flexibilitV for two-income and single-parent families. Day care programs, continued education, health plans, and even profit-sharing programs are encouraging employees to break the traditional pattern of short-term employment in this industry.

Competition

Competition can be identified as any restaurant business that offers a majority of food and beverage products and services that are directly competitive with those provided by your operation. Similarities in pricing structure are especially important to determine. Location, size, number of seats available, variety of facilities provided, theme, and cuisine are major factors that are surveyed in analyzing the competition.

The first step in establishing the competition is to determine a geographical radius in which the competition generally falls. There are always examples, however, of restaurants which, because of location or theme, are outside the general geographical radius but provide competition for your customers' business.

Overall factors that affect this radius are urban or rural setting, transportation routes or facilities, travel time, and location of your restaurant in relation to these factors. This information is available from libraries, city or town halls, chambers of commerce, and vocational schools and colleges.

It has been determined that the average customer will generally confine travel time to a restaurant to 30 to 45 minutes, resulting in a roundtrip time of 1 to 1½ hours. Laws concerning driving under the influence of alcohol have a major impact on the travel time some customers will allow when selecting a restaurant.

Interpreting the market survey

Understanding the key factors to be assessed in interpreting market survey information is essential to use this major marketing tool effectively.

Community needs

Primary to any decision involving developing or changing a food service operation is accurately determining the need for a new restaurant or changes in a restaurant in the community as a whole. The general economic health of the community is an essential indicator of what the response to different styles of food service operations will be.

Customer needs

Demographic information on a potential customer base can be broken down into the following demographic categories:

1. Age
2. Average income
3. Family size
4. Sex
5. Marital status
6. Occupation
7. Level of education

Segmentation is the breakdown of information into categories. It allows management to identify key factors about potential customers which would make them a more effective target market. To complete the exercise, management determines some common characteristics which identify their customer base. For example, customers may be light or heavy alcoholic beverage drinkers, sportsoriented, frequent travelers, casual or sophisticated in their dining habits. The combination of consumer characteristics and demographic information will create a customer profile that will identify a target market profile:

Customer profile + Demographic information = Target market.

This target market profile can now be broken down further into a segmentation of the frequency of customer use. The frequency with which a customer will return to a restaurant is a good indication of his or her reaction to marketing efforts. The pattern of use of a restaurant also provides additional marketing information for the customer profile.

Tools for measuring this information are often indicated by the method of payment that is most commonly used and the purpose of the customer's use of the restaurant. Restaurant operators who develop customer mailing lists can qualify their users by categories and target specific mailings and promotional activities to them. The three general categories are: heavy user, medium user, and light user.

By combining such additional information as family size, average check amount, beverage consumption, and purpose of visit these customers can be targeted for specific marketing efforts. A major identification of a segment of the market concerns what customer needs management can identify and create products and/or services to fulfill.

The fastest-growing segment of the food service industry is takeout. A combination of changes in the family profile, work patterns, and eating styles has increased the demand for high-quality food products that can be purchased fully or partially prepared and taken home for consumption. The profile of this customer might be the following:

Family size: 2-4

Average age: 35

Sex: female

Average income: medium to upper

Frequency: heavy user

Method of payment: check or credit card

Profession: career-oriented

Management can also use this information as the basis for future plans and decisions about changes in concepts, promotional activities, menu programs, hours of operation, and staffing.

Labour

By comparing increases or decreases in availability of labour with forecasts you will also be able to perceive how well you will be able to fill the labour requirements of your restaurant. The percentages of available labour within age ranges indicate the type of average employee you will have. High school students turn over quickly but have a high energy level. College students are seasonal and transient. Older employees are reliable and interested in their jobs. Their employment records are stronger than those of the other two groups. This population group is also more receptive to lower wage scales because this is a second income in many cases supplementing pensions and social security payments. Training programs provide an instant pool of employable personnel as well as a resource for training your employees.

Competition

The current trend toward company-owned units of corporate chains rather than franchises provides professional marketing information to independent owners and managers. Southwest Cafes, Inc., offers five different Mexican theme restaurants. Each restaurant concept answers the need of a different target market. Some offer higher-priced menu items and full service dining. Others offer midrange pricing with an appropriate menu item selection. Yet another offers a quick-serve atmosphere with low-range menu pricing. Interior decor and seating match the level of menu item selections and range of pricing.

By recognizing which market this company is trying to reach in establishing new restaurants, management can incorporate this information into their new development strategies. A thorough survey of the competition also allows management to compare menu item listings and prices. This comparison often reveals market saturation of cuisine trends, dining styles, and theme concepts.

By comparing the number of available customers with the current competition management can assess how competition could affect future business and decide whether the community will support the restaurant concepts and changes being envisioned. Market saturation of direct theme and menu ideas provides management with the opportunity to create a different approach to the original plans or change to different dining styles and levels of cuisine.

2

Restaurant Management Careers

The food service industry offers a dynamic spectrum of job opportunities at all levels of employment, from hourly wage staff to key management. These opportunities exist in work environments that range from small independent restaurant settings to corporate offices. Locations all over the world allow food service career professionals to select living environments for themselves and their families suited to individual life-style needs. Positions are also available in a variety of workplaces ranging from 24-hour commercial food service operations to contract feeding programs that function during normal business hours, 5 days a week. Teaching positions at secondary and post secondary schools, colleges, and universities offer the opportunity to apply industry experience and knowledge in the classroom. The operations management of the food service industry requires the skills of accountants, designers, tele-communications experts, real estate specialists, lawyers, and other professionals.

Career development is a lifelong program of personal growth toward objectives that range from financial to life-style goals. Identifying a career path in the food service industry requires a thorough understanding of all of the available opportunities. In addition, it is necessary to assess an individual's skills, strengths, and weaknesses to evaluate how well suited he or she is to meet the many and varied demands of this industry.

Entrepreneurship

Entrepreneurs are those individuals who have identified a need, have determined a product or service to answer that need, and are willing to expend the effort and financial commitment necessary to bring that product or service to market. The restaurant industry has historically provided an opportunity for entrepreneurs of all capabilities to fulfil their need to own their own business. Howard Johnson, Bill Marriott, Anthony Athanis, and Michael Hurst are just a few of the internationally recognized names of entrepreneurial restaurateurs. In every city and town there are entrepreneurial restaurant owners who represent a major source of employment and service in their community. Their contributions to the well-being of their communities reach far beyond financial investments.

Identifying yourself as an entrepreneur requires an evaluation of your ability to take risks. New business startups require long hours of hard work which often is not initially compensated while family and personal life is pushed aside. Entrepreneurs must be willing to accept failure as part of the process of developing ideas and concepts. Failure at one level often becomes the stepping stone to eventual success.

Entrepreneurs must have the following characteristics:

- High motivation
- Physical capability to work long hours
- Ability to accept advice
- Willingness to change direction when necessary
- Effective communication skill
- Creativity and spontaneity

Marketing entrepreneurial ideas

The first phase of the marketing cycle is to identify a need in the marketplace. Innovative entrepreneurs create new products or services to meet these needs. Creative imitation entrepreneurs redesign an existing product or service. Both styles of entrepreneurship are particularly adaptable to food service products and services. An example of creative innovation is the development of a ribless beef, pork, and chicken rib by Designer Foods in Wilmington, Delaware. A customer need was identified for a barbequed rib that could be eaten without using the fingers. Constant complaints were made about the problem of handling a messy product covered with sauce. Designer Foods, under the entrepreneurial leadership of Gene Gagliardi, developed a food processing method to shave the meat off the bone and blend it in such a way that it binds together without artificial ingredients.

The blended meat is then put through a meat processor that extrudes it to form an established portion size similar in appearance to a rack of ribs. When the product is appropriately sauced, it is packaged by a process called *cryovacing*, which extends product shelf life. The ribless meat product can be microwaved, oven processed, or grilled.

An example of creative imitation is the Dove Bar ice cream product. The company identified the need for a gourmet chocolate-covered ice cream product on a stick. Using a high butter fat content ice cream and an equally high quality chocolate, the company created a line of ice cream sticks boxed and priced in the range of $1.50 to $2.00 per bar.

The restaurant customer is being introduced daily to food products that have been flavoured, textured, shaped, preportioned, and preprepared during the manufacturing process in ways that reduce preparation labor, waste, cooking time, and costs.

The development of each of these products is part of an entrepreneurial marketing effort by food manufacturers to meet the needs of restaurateurs to reduce costs and increase profits.

Prospective entrepreneurs can prepare for a career in the food service industry through a combination of education and industry experience. After high school, an individual can identify various colleges and universities offering specific programs in entrepreneurship.

Gaining job experience by working directly in the determined interest area is necessary to develop a thorough understanding of the operational activities of a business as well as the paths of work and communication that must be followed by both employees and manage-ment. Entrepreneurs who have gained an education in their field of interest often supplement their knowledge with specific business and industry-related courses to increase their ability to develop, market, and operate products and businesses.

Food service career path

Food service careers are broken down into three primary levels: entry, middle management, and management. Restaurant businesses classify job positions as production, service, or management. Training and educational criteria vary at each level. Wages for hourly employees are often controlled by state and federal regulations. Representative salaries for management positions fluctuate regionally across the United States.

Entry-level positions food production

- Line Cook

- Baker's Helper
- Prep Worker
- Dishwasher
- Service
- Host/Hostess
- Bartender
- Waiter/Waitress
- Counter Worker (quick serve)
- Cafeteria Server
- Bus Person

Middle management food production

- Chef
- Pastry Chef
- Kitchen Manager
- Cafeteria Manager

Service

- Beverage Manager
- Purchasing Agent
- Banquet (Catering) Manager
- Assistant Restaurant Manager
- Head Bartender
- Maitre d' Hotel (Head Waiter)
- Dining Room Captain

Management

- Owner/Operator

- Food Service Director
- Personnel Director
- Controller
- Training Director

Wage rates for hourly employees are based on minimum wage regulations. In the food service industry positions which include tips as part of employee compensation have lower minimum wage requirements than other positions.

Compensation packages

Compensation packages include benefits as well as salary. These benefits are often nontaxable, such as medical insurance and education. Other benefits include future income-producing opportunities such as pension plans and profit-sharing programs.

Stock options also allow employees to purchase single shares of stock directly from the company without paying the broker fees normally associated with stock purchases and sales. The value of a compensation package depends on the needs of the individual. Single persons do not need comprehensive family health and dental plans but may see considerable value in stock option benefits.

Profit sharing is a benefit used by management to create employee incentive to increase quality control and profit. If the company is not highly profitable, then employees may not feel that this benefit has real value for them. On the other hand, if the company is highly profitable, this benefit could result in financial bonuses at the end of the company's fiscal year.

Training and education

Education for food service industry related jobs often

begins with high school courses in the home economics department or in a specified career track in a vocational school. These programs, combined with job experience, often give future restaurant managers their initial training and interest in the field.

Training

Training for food production jobs is often found in established apprenticeship programs in hotels and restaurants. Under the direction of certified chefs and food service directors, apprenticeship programs are administered by professional associations such as the American Culinary Federation. Through the program, cooks work with certified chefs to learn the job skills for each of the stations in the kitchen.

When they have satisfactorily mastered the required skills, they are awarded a certificate of achievement that can be applied to their own professional certification. Job pay in these situations is usually less than regular wages to compensate for instruction.

Professional certification programs available for food service management personnel include such specific areas as sanitation, food cost control, and employee supervision. These are administered as part of courses which are offered at area schools and colleges with hospitality-restaurant management programs. They are also available in correspondence form from recognized educational programs representing the food service industry.

Management certification programs covering broad areas of food service knowledge and experience represent industry acknowledgment and professional skill achievement. By gaining such certification an individual is accorded the privilege of using the program title initials after his or her professional name. A certified food service executive uses the initials CFE, a certified food and beverage executive CFBE, and a certified master chef CMC.

Culinary

Culinary degree programs combine food service management and culinary arts courses with required liberal arts components. These are generally associate degree of science programs that require the completion of approximately 60 credit hours. The normal amount of time taken to complete these programs is 2 academic years. Some form of practical internship or cooperative work experience is required to complete this degree.

Restaurant management and institutional food service management

Restaurant management and institutional food service management are the general 2-year core curriculums for both 2-year and 4-year degree programs in food service management. Students determine whether they will focus their attention on commercial restaurant management or institutional and business food service management.

Depending on the course of instruction, these programs include business-related and general management courses as well as food service management and culinary arts skills. They usually require an internship or cooperative work experience component. These 4-year programs award a bachelor of science degree and require completion of approximately 120 credit hours.

Career choice

Identifying a career path requires an individual to assess his or her skills and abilities objectively and realistically as well as to identify career and personal goals and objectives. This process of self-assessment often necessitates input from counsellors, teachers, and employers, who can give considerable insight into a person's work habits, potential for achievement, and personality. Their contributions can be valuable in helping to determine whether goals and objectives are realistic. One of the most important characteristics needed for successful self-assessment is an overall orientation toward a career field. All managerial positions require interaction with other people, particularly in restaurant businesses.

Marketing in a restaurant operation is an essential management function that directly affects the success of a business. Restaurant businesses directly produce and provide customers goods and services that satisfy the need for food, beverage, and entertainment. The producer is directly accessible to the consumer, creating a proximity that allows restaurant management to identify and respond to customer needs.

The consumer wants to inform the producer in the retail marketing chain of needs that could be satisfied or changes that would make a product more salable. In order to do this, it is necessary either to pass backward through the chain of product distribution or to find a way of reaching the producer directly The restaurant distribution chart gives the producer and consumer direct access to one another.

At the time that a decision is made to develop a restaurant business, it is necessary to identify and understand consumer needs. Marketing methods and techniques that are essential to developing a good marketing program are the marketing cycle, the food service marketing mix, and the marketing campaign. Identifying marketing opportunities is the key to successful product/service development.

The marketing cycle

The marketing cycle is a series of four steps that are used to create and evaluate products and services. These steps as outlined:

1. Identify consumer needs
2. Develop products and services to meet needs
3. Generate consumer interest to purchase or use product/service
4. Evaluate financial success and consumer satisfaction.

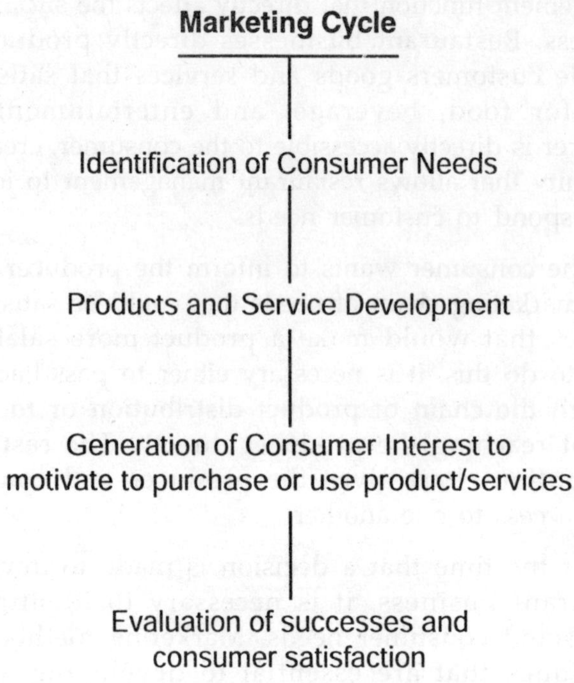

Fig. 1: Restaurant industry marketing distribution chart

These steps must be performed in the sequence indicated to bring a product or service to market successfully.

Identify consumer needs

A consumer need is identified when management recognizes a service or product that is not currently being offered. Need is usually recognized when a product/ service is requested by the consumer or offered by other restaurant operations. Healthy dining is an excellent example of a customer need that has been identified by food service operations.

Restaurant managers use the resources of local hospitals to create menu items which are developed to meet nutritional guidelines. A number of restaurant associations across the United States have developed healthy dining programs.

Develop a product or service

Developing a product or service to meet consumer needs requires that management thoroughly understand consumer needs and accurately identify the perceived value of the product or service. It is essential that the selling price be determined before the product specifications are outlined. The cost of producing the product will directly affect the selling price. If consumers are not willing to pay the price, then the product will not be financially successful.

Generate consumer interest

Generating consumer interest is achieved primarily by applying market research information to determine a target market at which is directed a variety of interest--generating advertising media. To achieve the desired response from the target market, it is necessary to develop a marketing campaign. Marketing campaigns plan a series of events, promotions, and advertising placements. The objective of these activities is to reach established goals of increased revenues and/or customer counts.

Evaluate success

The success of a product or service is evaluated in terms of both financial and customer satisfaction objectives. Financial success is judged by determining whether management's original financial objectives for the product were met. Customer satisfaction is gauged by analysing customer reaction to the product or service. A good way of recording customer reactions is to provide comment cards.

To use this marketing information effectively, management needs to establish a policy of sharing the comments with employees and responding directly to them. Favourable and critical comments should always be passed along to staff. Sharing problems identified by customers at general staff meetings often produces solutions that are employee-generated. Acknowledging customer complaints and providing an incentive to return increase the perception of professionalism and interest in the restaurant.

The food service mix

To set the marketing cycle in motion, three major factors regarding the product must be established. These factors, called the marketing mix, determine where the product will be presented to the customer, how the customer will be informed about the product, and what price the product will be assigned.

To address the food service industry, however, the traditional marketing mix must be adjusted to incorporate the service component that is essential to food service products. Food service products, especially in restaurant settings, require an element of service in order to reach the customer, changing the first marketing mix element to Product-Service. Presentation incorporates factors such as theme and staffing as well as location.

Price is an important factor in the presentation of a food product, often determining customer acceptability. Promotion includes the application of marketing methods and the communication skills required to sell food product directly to the customer.

Marketing opportunities

Successful entrepreneurs and marketing specialists are individuals who recognize an opportunity to satisfy a need or create a product or service. Their ability to do so is often aligned with circumstances that indicate the probability of success. These circumstances are primarily related to demographic or environmental issues.

The demographic issue identified as having the major impact on the food service industry will be the aging of the baby boom generation, which will increase the average age of the entire population. According to the Bureau of Labor Statistics: Consumers in the age bracket between 34 and 54 years old spend over 30% more on foodservice than other age groups. This segment of the population will grow by 11.3 million individuals (a 32% increase) by the year 2000.

The United States will experience a period of unprecedented personal wealth over the next twenty years, directly associated with this demographic transition. Services that make life easier will experience gains. The use of restaurants and other food service operations is no longer an extravagant drain on the family budget but a necessity. In 1991 food service industry sales were over $256 billion, accounting for 45 percent of all dollars spent on food. This figure may reach 50 percent by the year 2000.

The demographics that can and are affecting the food service industry merit continual review by owners and managers, who must be able to observe, analyse, and forecast shifts and trends that will affect their customers and business. Often referred to as external environmental factors, demographic characteristics are of several types.

Some of the factors currently having a profound impact on the restaurant industry in the sociocultural category are life-style changes, family arrangements, and changing women's roles. Economic factors include unemployment levels as well as energy sources and costs.

Competitive factors are number and strength of competitors, market growth, and market share. Radical economic changes in the 1990s are affecting the entire world economy.

Restaurant managers should seek out and use information that interprets and indicates how these factors will affect a community to develop a marketing plan. Market survey information often provides strong indicators of how a community is reacting to national and world trends. As demographic changes reach the community level, managers can identify opportunities to react with products or services which reflect the needs of their customer base. Market research information often provides the data to support the development of marketing opportunities.

1991 meal period highlights

Breakfast

— More than one out of five (20.7 percent) of all individuals over eight years old consumed a commercially prepared breakfast at least once during a week.

— On the average, individuals consumed 0.5 breakfasts away from home in a week.

— The average individual skipped 1.6 breakfasts in one week, making breakfast the most frequently skipped meal.

Lunch

— Almost six out of ten (56.8 percent) individuals ate lunch prepared away from home at least once a week. This makes lunch the meal most frequently consumed away from home.

— Individuals consumed, on the average, 2.1 lunches away from home per week.

— The average individual skipped lunch 0.6 times in a week.

Dinner

— Among individuals over age eight, 53.5 percent consumed at least one commercially prepared dinner in a seven-day period.

— The average individual consumed 1.2 dinners away from home in a week.

— Individuals skipped, on average, only 0.1 dinners in a one-week period.

Market research

Market research information can be gathered from a variety of sources. Competition surveys offer information about the average check, menu items, beverage prices, and facilities of restaurants that are in direct competition for the same customer. Understanding how much the customer is willing to pay for a product or service in a competitive setting gives management a strong indication of acceptable pricing.

Management can use market research information on average per person check totals to help identify which category of overall sales volume matches their operation. By comparing national average checks with current sales volumes, consumer spending trends can be analysed to find out whether the customer's perceived value of menu items is higher than what is currently being charged. The results of interpreting this type of market research information could also cause management to change the focus or concept of the overall menu program. Further analysis of the current marketplace for restaurant dollars focuses on research concerning the composition of the average American household. By understanding how households allocate food service dollars, management can identify the target market for marketing efforts for their operation.

The marketing campaign

The marketing campaign is the application of the marketing cycle phase, generating customer interest. Creating promotions, planning advertising materials, and developing a formal media program are elements of a marketing campaign. The food service marketing mix provides the information that is the foundation of any marketing campaign. The development stage of a marketing campaign requires establishing the most effective way of creating customer interest. A variety of methods for advertising and promotion are available.

Internal methods of promotion include special events incorporating holidays or speciality cuisines. In-house advertising can be accomplished by table tents and cards, posters, banners, and a server communication program. The most effective use of advertising media for a restaurant business focuses on newspaper ads and radio time. Newspaper ads are generally timed to appear on days of the week which have been identified as those when readers are looking for entertainment information. The same principle applies to identifying radio time that reaches the established target market.

Community goodwill is an important component in generating customer interest. A business's involvement in local activities of all types creates good public relations and often free advertising in the form of media coverage.

The final phase of the marketing campaign is the evaluation of the success of the program. Success is determined by how well management's objectives are met. If the primary objective is to increase sales, success is measured by the amount of increase in revenues. If the objective is to increase customer attendance, success is measured by the total increase in customer counts.

Management establishes a return rate target goal and methods by which to track it. If the return rate falls below the goal level, then measures are taken to evaluate product and service in order to increase repeat customers. An effective marketing plan is generally developed around an established outline. Owners and managers who are not familiar with formal marketing plans would be advised to seek professional assistance.

3

Hotel Operations

As a hotel department, accounting is far more important to management success than the articles included here would suggest. In the hierarchy of most major hotel firms, the chief accountant, or controller, as this manager is more often called, ranks among the top two or three decision makers. The importance of this job is suggested by the observation that many traditional hotel departments have been reorganized so major functions now report to the controller's office. The prime example of this is the front office, where previously the front office manager supervised the activities of the night audit staff, cashiers, and other front desk clerks.

Increasingly, hotel firms are transferring the responsibility for night audits and cashiers to the accounting office, with the ultimate responsibility for these information-gathering and controlling functions resting with the hotel controller. Another increasingly important department in the hotel is one that coordinates and supervises all the electronic data processing (EDP) or management information systems (MIS).

In many instances, EDP and MIS functions are now also the responsibility of the hotel controller. This recognizes the training and the ability of hotel controllers to provide for the structured accumulation, storage, and reporting of data in forms that are most useful to the operating departments and other executives of the hotel.

The success of hotel firms in the modern era will depend on how well they manage, control, and utilize the information that is available to them for their own operations. Managers also need to develop other sources of information in the business environment that affect their regulatory structure and their competition.

The hotel controller

The 1989 survey on hotel controller was based on a questionnaire mailed to 750 members of the International Association of Hospitality Accountants (IAHA) who were identified as working in hotel accounting positions. We received a total of 319 responses, representing a response rate of 42.5 percent.

More than 90 percent of the controllers who responded have at least an associate's degree and nearly 20 percent have at least a master's degree. Those findings are similar to those of the 1983 study. The areas of study that our respondents pursued while in college are also similar to those identified in 1983, with over 50 percent having concentrated on accounting.

A significant change, however, was the increase in the number of individuals who were enrolled in hospitality management programs. In 1983, a mere 8 percent of the controllers listed "hotel/ restaurant administration" as their college major, while in the current survey that number more than doubled, to over 17 percent. Such a dramatic increase may mean that more hospitality program graduates now view the controller's position as a career track or as a steppingstone to top management.

The shift can be viewed also from the demand side—perhaps hotel companies now recognize the value of hospitality management training and operations experience in the controller's position.

In 1989, the most frequently cited areas of knowledge were computers, cash management, and internal controls, each of which was claimed by more than 90 percent of our study sample. As with the 1983 survey, although cash management was considered important by more than 90 percent of the respondents, controllers do not appear to have significant authority over the two critical cash management functions of investing (46.4 percent) and borrowing funds (20.4 percent). More controllers became familiar with taxes and computers between 1983 and 1989. The controllers' knowledge of taxes went from 60 to 75 percent of respondents reporting tax knowledge, and the percentage familiar with computers rose almost 30 percentage points (from 70 percent to 97 percent).

In the latest survey we asked the controllers to grade themselves on two new areas of expertise: Financial Accounting Standards Board (FASB) pronouncements and risk management. Only 18 percent were up to date with the FASB, while 36 percent said "yes" to having knowledge of risk management. Also, "auditing" and "internal control" were listed as separate categories in 1989, whereas they were combined for the 1983 survey.

More than 90 percent of the respondents indicated that they have responsibility for such standard accounting functions as general accounting, receivables, payables, and payroll, a finding virtually identical to that in 1983. Other major areas of responsibility shared by most controllers include night and income audits, cashiers, and food and beverage controls. There are some indications that controllers are becoming increasingly involved with the operational aspects of their hotels. More than 50 percent of the respondents indicated that their responsibilities included purchasing, receiving, and storage (inventory).

The number of respondents responsible for the storage function increased 18 points from 1983 to 1989, going from 34 percent to more than 52 percent, and a purchasing function was claimed by 60 percent of the respondents, which is ten points greater than in 1983. Responsibility for hotel security, the least commonly shared function among the controllers, more than doubled in the last six years, growing from 9 percent in 1983 to almost 22 percent in the current study.

The controllers' role in electronic data processing (EDP) and computer system management grew by leaps and bounds during the 1980s. In 1989, more than 87 percent of the respondents indicated responsibility for the computer systems used for accounting functions. Additionally, 58 percent indicated responsibility for front office and reservations system computers—systems clearly not under the umbrella of traditional accounting functions. In the 1983 study, we asked just one question about responsibility for EDP, and 52 percent of the controllers indicated that they had some responsibility for EDP. It's possible, however, that the 1983 finding is understated due to the vagueness of the question. In any event, it's clear that over the years computer-oriented responsibilities have escalated sharply. That conclusion is certainly consistent with the proliferation of electronic data-processing systems in all aspects of hotel operations.

The majority of controllers reported responsibility of tax returns, cash management, and beverage controls. A substantial percentage (more than 36 percent of the respondents in each case) also indicated responsibility for internal auditors, investments, and risk management.

Our supposition that hotel controllers are increasingly becoming involved with all aspects of hotel operations and, as a result, are viewed as valuable members of the top management team, seems well founded. Further evidence of this professional leap upward is found by looking at the executive committee involvement of controllers.

Overwhelming majorities of controllers are involved with such key management committees as compensation, executive, long-range planning, training, and risk management. By contrast, in the 1983 survey, only 23 percent of the controllers were on compensation committees (versus 75 percent in 1989), and only 41 percent were involved with long-range planning (versus 94 percent in 1989).

There were insufficient salary increments in the questionnaire used for the 1983 study, and that flaw caused some confusion in the results. That problem was rectified in the current study by incorporating a wide range of salary increments—from under $20,000 to over $80,000. The symmetrical distribution of salaries suggests that this time we successfully captured the compensation picture. Our results show that not only have salaries kept pace with inflation over the years, but that the distributions have been skewed significantly upward. For example, the lower increments (under $30,000) include fewer than 12 percent of the 1989 respondents compared to 32 percent in 1983. Similarly, the range of $30,000-$39,900 has dropped from 39 percent to 30 percent. At the same time, the high end has expanded. The top five increments of the 1989 study (salaries greater than $40,000) comprise more than 58 percent of the respondents, which is more than double the figure for the same salary range in 1983 (29 percent). As one might expect, experience and the specific characteristics of a controller's company or hotel affect his or her salary. Here there are no surprises: The higher the controller's position, the higher the median salary; the larger the hotel (whether measured by number of rooms or annual room sales), the higher the median salary; the higher the level of education obtained, the higher the median salary. Such results are very similar to those from the 1983 study.

Bonus points

Typically, salary structures for top management personnel include provisions for bonuses. The number of controllers receiving bonuses in the 1989 study was about seven out of ten, up from slightly more than six out of ten in 1983. The median bonus in 1989 was between 11 and 20 percent of a controller's salary.

While many different factors contribute to whether or not a controller will earn a bonus, the most common basis for issuing a bonus to a controller was whether the enterprise met its profit objectives. That standard affected almost 60 percent of controllers in 1989. Other bonus determining factors may include one or more of the following: meeting sales objectives, increasing profits over those from the previous year, achieving personal objectives, accounts receivable performance, cash flow, employee satisfaction, and corporate profits. The availability of fringe benefits for controllers in the current study is quite similar to the findings of the 1983 study.

Internal auditing

As a company grows and becomes more complex, its owners are no longer able to perform all the managerial tasks necessary to ensure that it is operating properly. There is an increasing need to have independent evaluations of the firm's activities that will provide a review of financial operations, an examination of internal controls, or even an evaluation of the economy, efficiency, and effectiveness of organizational procedures.

The scope of these evaluations frequently extends to nonfinancial aspects of the company such as an appraisal of the degree of compliance by employers and employees with the company's code of ethics or perhaps the organization's compliance with provisions of the Equal Employment Opportunity Act. The multiple needs of most modern -businesses, government, and not-for-profit organizations for those types of independent evaluations have led to the establishment of internal audit functions within their organizational structure. Because of their technical competence in accounting, auditing, and related business fields, internal auditors can and should conduct these independent appraisals.

The Institute of Internal Auditors, the professional association of internal auditors, defines, in its membership materials, internal auditing as "an independent appraisal function established within an organization to examine and evaluate its activities as a service to the organization." This definition requires an explanation of key words, as follows:

1. "Independent" means the audit work is not restricted in regard to its scope, effectiveness of review, or the reporting of findings and conclusions.
2. "Appraisal" includes fact finding, evaluation, and conclusions.
3. "Activities" include both financial and nonfinancial activities of the organization.
4. "Service" means providing assistance to the organization.
5. Lastly, "organization" includes operational personnel, boards of directors and their committees, and stockholders.

Focus of internal auditing

The focus of the internal audit function is control. In fact, the internal audit function is a control designed to appraise the effectiveness of other controls. Internal control has been defined by the American Institute of Certified Public Accountants (AICPA) as "the plan of organization and all of the coordinate methods and measures within a business to safeguard its assets, check the accuracy and reliability of its accounting data, promote operational efficiency and encourage adherence to prescribed managerial policies".

The controls used to safeguard an organization's assets, such as locks to secure assets, restricting access to certain assets, and checking the accuracy and reliability of its accounting data by, for instance, review of the bank reconciliation, are referred to as accounting controls. Historically, internal auditors have focused their attention on these activities.

The objectives of promoting operating efficiency and encouraging adherence to prescribed managerial policies have been referred to as administrative controls. Internal auditing over the past several years has been expanded to include the evaluation of administrative controls. In other words, a business uses an internal auditor not only to determine that credit sales and subsequent cash received are recorded properly and cash is properly "secured" but to determine if the operations resulting in sales are efficient and in compliance with the pertinent laws. The role of the internal auditor has been enlarged due to the expanding oversight of various government agencies and the passage of new laws. Today's hospitality firm has to satisfy many different agencies at all levels of government.

The business is required to comply with complex regulations issued by taxing authorities, health and safety authorities, fair trade administrators, equal rights and affirmative action units, pension plan agencies, to name a few, while meeting a host of provisions regarding licensing of activities and the conduct of business operations.

Functional role of the internal auditor

The question often arises as to how an internal audit staff can conduct audits that require such a wide range of knowledge in so many different areas. The principal reasons that professional auditors can successfully do this are:

1. Highly qualified personnel, professionally designated as CPAs (certified public accountants), CIAs (certified internal auditors), and CMAs (certified management accountants), comprise a significant portion of the staffs of successful internal audit departments. Auditors maintain and improve their competence through continuing education programs.
2. Many internal audit departments utilize a team concept in building their staffs. This concept includes persons from various academic disciplines (accounting, auditing, finance, computer sciences, management, marketing, and others) who provide a synergistic effect.
3. Consultants or specialists are employed as needed to supply additional technical assistance.
4. Internal auditors are highly trained to use standards (desirable benchmarks) against which they compare actual organizational performance.

The internal auditor is not part of the operations team. Even though it may seem to be more efficient to use internal auditors to determine account number assignments or to decide when an expenditure should be capitalized, internal auditors must maintain their independence if they are to serve as appraisers of operating activities. Secondly, the internal auditor has a staff assignment rather than a line position. Line managers have the responsibility for operations, and this should not be shifted to the internal auditor.

The findings and recommendations of the internal auditor are advisory and should be implemented by line personnel based on their merits to the operation as determined by the line personnel. In order for the internal auditing function to be independent, that is, properly detached from operations and the functional staff groups such as accounting, finance, and marketing, the internal auditors often answer to the top management such as the chief financial officer, the operating executive, or even the audit committee of the board of directors.

Recent research on internal auditors in major lodging chains revealed that:

1. 19.4 percent reported to the controller.
2. 32.3 percent reported to the senior financial officers.
3. 16.1 percent reported to a corporate executive and the board.
4. 6.5 percent reported to the board.
5. 32 percent reported to the audit committee of the board.

The independence (ability to make objective audit decisions unaffected by influence from the activity audited) of internal auditors is affected primarily by two things: (1) the organizational level to which the auditor reports, and (2) the professional training and mindset of objectivity of the internal auditor.

Internal auditing activities

Internal auditing activities may be divided into four broad categories by the financial and managerial data each examines. The four major activities are:

1. Checking compliance with internal controls and procedures.

2. Checking compliance with applicable laws and procedures.
3. Determining whether the firm's resources are being used efficiently.
4. Determining whether the firm's resources are being used effectively.

The internal auditing activities pertaining to internal controls would generally include such procedures as reviewing the bank reconciliation (financial data) and determining that there is adequate separation of duties in the handling of cash transactions (nonfinancial data).

This major activity area received increased emphasis with the passage of the Foreign Corrupt Practices Act of 1977, which mandated that businesses have adequate internal accounting controls. The activities included under checking compliance with applicable laws and procedures also pertain to financial and nonfinancial data. For example, the financial aspect includes the review of the company's federal tax return to determine compliance with the Internal Revenue Code.

A nonfinancial aspect is determining whether the food and beverage operation is in compliance with, local health department regulations. The internal auditing activities oriented to the efficient use of organizational resources would include conducting analytical reviews of various assets such as accounts receivables and inventories (financial data) and determining the efficiency of the firm's marketing efforts (nonfinancial data). Finally, internal auditing activities evaluating the effective use of the firm's resources would include determining whether the return on investment (ROI) for a property is above the organization's hurdle rate (financial) and determining the effectiveness of community service projects (nonfinancial).

Exhibit 1 illustrates the administrative control model used to exercise control over a typical hospitality operation. Management prescribes operating procedures that lead to actual output or performance by the firm. Management also has the responsibility of adopting standards of performance or output that they believe to be desirable and attainable.

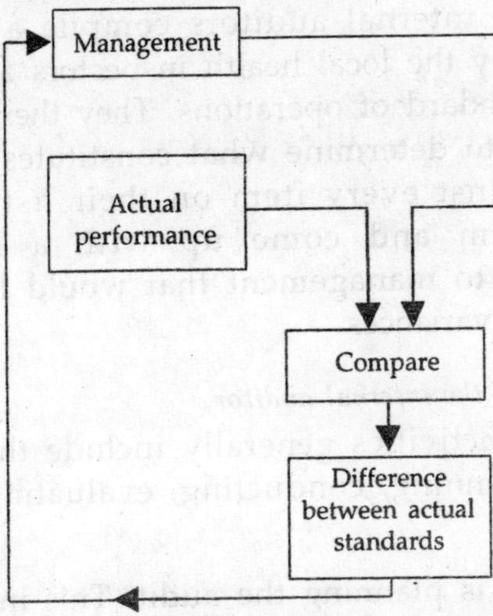

Exhibit 1: Adminidtrative control model

In the model, actual results are compared with the standards and the difference between the two (called a variance) is fed back through managerial performance reports to that level of management capable of controlling the operating procedure. When actual performance exceeds the standard of performance, the variance is called favourable. When the standard exceeds the actual, the variance is unfavourable.

Under normal operating conditions, managers will analyse significant variances to determine if below standard operation exists. They then review operating procedures to determine if changes are required to bring actual operations to the level established by standards.

Occasionally, they may revise standards that are obsolete or in error. Internal auditors use this model to analyse operating efficiency and effectiveness of the organization. They have also learned to apply the model to an extremely wide range of audit situations where what a firm is doing in any function is compared to the desired level (standard) for that function.

For example, internal auditors compile a list of procedures used by the local health inspectors and use this list as the standard of operations. They then apply audit procedures to determine what constitutes actual performance against every item on their list. They analyse each item and come up with a list of recommendations to management that would lead to elimination of any variances.

Technical approach of the internal auditor

Internal auditing activities generally include the four major steps of planning, conducting, evaluating, and reporting.

The first step is planning the audit. This includes gaining knowledge about the operational entity to be reviewed, determining audit objectives, accumulating all pertinent data, conducting an on-site survey, and preparing the audit program. The on-site survey is conducted at the hospitality facility location and includes discussion with the responsible manager and other key personnel and reviewing policies and procedures.

Planning the audit includes detailing the procedures to be followed and delineating the steps to be performed to meet the audit objectives. Though the audit program is prepared prior to conducting the review, new evidence and changes in audit staff may require changes in the audit program as the review progresses. From the planning phase, the internal auditor moves to conducting the audit, sometimes referred to as the verification phase. The actual audit procedures used to obtain the necessary data vary by type of audit.

Common procedures used and an example of each are as follows:

Procedure	*Example*
Comparing	Comparison of actual room sales to budgeted room sales and reviewing explanations for significant differences.
Vouching	Reviewing suppliers' invoices to support amounts recorded as food purchases.
Confirming	Having food purveyors verify the amount of unpaid invoices at the end of the year.
Scanning	Visually reviewing cash register tapes to determine if the number of sales transactions and voided transactions on the restaurant's cash register equals the number of completed or voided server checks for a given time period.
Analysing	A comparison of an operating department's labour costs to its sales for several one-week periods throughout the year.
Inquiring	Obtaining a reasonable explanation from the head of the maintenance department as to why maintenance costs

	exceeded the budget for the month by 15 percent.
Observing	Observing the complete processing of a guest's food order from the recording by the server to delivery of food to the guest to determine the efficiency of the process.
Recomputing	Adding the cost of food inventory items to verify the computer total.

The evaluation phase is critical to drawing conclusions that are the basis for management decisions. The scope of this phase may be best understood by answering these questions.

1. How good is the result presently being achieved? The focus may be how well a procedure has been complied as a measure of efficiency or effectiveness.
2. Why is the result what it is? Related to the first question is the evaluation of why the results are as they are and perhaps why they are not better.
3. Finally, what could be done to achieve better results in the future?

The final phase is reporting the results of the audit. The report summarizes what has been accomplished and makes the results available to executive level management.

The night audit

Hotels have always needed methods for keeping guest accounts up to date and ready for submission when guests check out. Because check-outs usually occur early in the morning it has fallen upon the front office night shift—those people working from 11:00 PM to 7:00 AM—to accumulate all charges and credits guests have accrued and to prepare the bill for presentation. Over the years, the procedure has become known as the night audit, and the individual who performs it as the night auditor. As the size and complexity of hotels increased and the demands on the night auditor grew, the night audit procedure evolved from a relatively simple, handwritten process to the sophisticated electronic systems that even small hotels use today.

Part of the night audit procedure involves compiling the guest bill for presentation. These bills are the accounts receivable to the hotel and must be readied daily since guests might wish to look at their bill or check out at any time. There is, however, more to the night audit than just preparing guest bills. The main task, and the real "audit" portion of the process, is to reconcile all the accounts, ensuring that all charges are correctly posted (assigned) to the proper guest accounts.

Records of each hotel department's charges are forwarded to the night auditor, who compares what has been posted to the guest accounts with what was actually charged in the department. This process culminates in the auditor performing a trial balance of all the different guest accounts, thus ensuring that all accounting transactions relating to these accounts were handled correctly.

The reason that this has to be done nightly is simple. Since guest accounts must be kept current, a "normal" accounts receivable system that bills the individual at the end of a longer period (such as a month) would clearly be inadequate.

Most hotel operations would never consider this kind of billing procedure, because the ex-guests would be spread over a large geographical area, making collection difficult.

Additionally, even a small hotel would accumulate a large number of bills in a relatively short time. For example, a 250-room hotel that was 70 percent occupied during a month with only one person per room would generate 5,250 guestdays of business (250 × 30 × 0.7). If each guest stayed for three days, that would mean there would be 1,750 different bills (5,250/3) to prepare at the end of the month!

The original purpose of the night audit procedure was to ensure that the bills presented to guests were accurate and up to date. The accounts needed to be reconciled before the guest departed.

Since this was usually in the morning, and since the late-night shift at a front desk was usually quiet, it was logical that the procedure that became the night audit would be done at this time. It also allowed someone to post all the accounts that the guest accrued before the guest went to bed, including the charge for the room itself. By midnight, it could be assumed that everyone who was going to check into the hotel had. The accounting day would end with the closing of the last department, usually the lounge, and all charges for the day could be posted.

The history of the night audit procedure can be separated into three main categories: (1) the hand transcript, (2) the machine audit, and (3) the electronic audit. Each of the categories evolved as a necessary response to the increased size and complexity of hotel operations, alongside the development of new technologies to aid the night auditor. While these three categories evolved in the order presented, it should be remembered that there are a number of hotels today that use a hand transcript or machine audit and have, for good reasons, not completely adopted the latest technology.

The hand transcript

In the early days of hotels the hand transcript developed from the need for room clerks to account for the increasing number of guests hotels were accommodating. During the nineteenth century, hotels were growing rapidly in size, and it was no longer possible for a landlord or owner to perform all the tasks required as host. Traditionally, the desk of the smaller hotel, if there even was one, would close at night.

However, as the hotels became larger, the need for desk clerks and other employees increased, and the notion of a 24-hour front desk operation arose. Similarly, a need to keep track of guest accounts arose, since more and more establishments were allowing patrons to charge instead of requiring cash up front. It was no longer practical for accounts to be prepared when guests asked for them. Additionally, hoteliers in general were discovering the increased need for control over the monies that were being generated. As a consequence, the concept of the night audit, born out of these conditions, developed.

The original night audit was a handwritten, manually totalled list of guest accounts. On a large sheet of paper, or in a ledger book, individual guest accounts were arranged in rows, while the different departments that a guest could charge in were arranged in columns. After guest charges were accumulated and each individual bill was tabulated, the entries on the bills were transferred to the night audit transcript. Exhibit 1 provides an example of a typical hand transcript.

Both debit (charge) and credit (payment) entries were included. Row totals were calculated as debits minus credits equals amount due. Column totals were calculated and represented the total charges or credits for each department. In this fashion, the auditors would be able to verify each guest's bill by comparing it to the bill as originally created.

More importantly, the auditors could then compare the departmental totals with another set of totals prepared in the individual department.

Any discrepancies would have to be resolved. In essence, this was the true audit part of the night audit-to review the accounts as posted, and make sure they were all done correctly. Unfortunately, several other tasks were asked of the auditors which limited their time and ability to actually "audit" the books. These will be discussed in the next section. What is important is that the basic function of the auditor, and the underlying methodology of how the audit works, has remained essentially unchanged as the audit process has evolved. The primary task of the night audit today is still to review the accounts, and isolate and remedy any mistakes.

The Machine Audit

As electric cash registers became more popular, specialized machines were developed for specialized purposes, one of which was a machine that would perform the mechanical aspects of the night audit. Perhaps the most famous of these were the series of posting machines built by the National Cash Register Company. Almost every front office manager or hotel manager who started a career from the 1930s to the present time has had experience on one or another of these machines.

The advantages of these machines were several. First, they would automatically total the charges or credits for each department, eliminating the need for hand calculations.

Second, the folio that is the permanent guest record could be processed through the machine, providing to the guest (and to the front office personnel) complete information on charges and credits during the guest's stay, including the date of the transaction, the department involved, the amount of the transaction, and the room number the charge was posted to. This "automated" approach eliminated much of the drudgery involved in the bookkeeping aspect of the audit and freed the auditors to spend more time on the audit portion of the job-finding mistakes and correcting them.

Third advantage of the machine was that each individual posting clerk could be controlled by having separate locks on the machine. Therefore, it was easier to monitor the activity at the front desk. This became especially important as hotels grew larger and the posting clerks were made responsible for posting charges to the guest accounts as they were accumulated during the day's operation. The goal was to require the night auditor to post as few charges as possible, thus freeing time to perform the actual audit.

A fourth advantage, and perhaps the most important from the standpoint of the night auditor, was the ability to print out a form referred to as the "D" card. The "D" card, was a special form that automatically totalled the entire day's activity. This gives departmental totals for all debit and credit transactions that were made on the posting machine.

This particular form was printed out while the night auditor was clearing the machine, or "zeroing out" the totals on the posting of the machine, making it ready for the next day's transactions. Obviously, this would only be done when all posting for the day had been completed. The "D" card naturally followed the "A," "B," "C," cards, which were individual shift totals for the posting clerks during the three eight-hour shifts each day. This system allowed for three levels of control to be placed on the employees involved in posting charges. The department cashiers could validate the charges made by the individual clerks in the departments.

The posting clerks could validate any charges coming from the various departments. The night auditor, who could validate the work of the posting clerks, was the only person who could reset the machine. Note, however, that this system did not apply when the night auditor posted accounts as well as verifying them. One other situation arose during the time that the posting/auditing machines developed. To this point all discussion has centered around the charges made by guests -staying at the hotel, or the transient guests. These accounts were grouped together in what came to be known as the transient ledger.

However, another entire category of guests existed: guests who were not currently staying in the hotel but were nevertheless allowed charging privileges. Originally, these individuals would probably have lived in the city where the hotel was and, as a result ' came to be known as city ledger guests. The city ledger accounts were, and still are, very similar to the standard type of accounts found in any retail store since it was easier to bill them than to bill the accounts of transient guests.

Moreover, since the majority of transactions in the hotels remained transient ledger accounts, the night auditor's function was expanded to include these charges as well. This simplified the bookkeeping process by having all charges funnel into one area. In general terms, then, the job of the night auditor would include the following steps:

1. Post any remaining departmental charges to their proper accounts, whether city or transient ledger.
2. Post all room charges, including tax, to their proper accounts.

3. Perform a trial balance of accounts, to ensure all accounts are posted correctly. Make any adjusting entries necessary.

4. Finalize the audit by clearing the machine and setting it for the next day.

5. Prepare any reports that management has requested.

There were problems associated with the machine audits. First, the machines would post to whatever accounts the posting clerks entered in them. This meant that posting to a wrong account, posting the wrong amount, and forgetting to post entirely were still problems. Additionally, since any posting made was now a part of the machine's accumulated total, making changes were not simply a matter of erasing the wrong number and replacing it with the correct one.

The Electronic Audit

The final type of audit, and the type in general usage in most types of hotels today, is the electronic audit. Essentially, this evolutionary trend is an offshoot of the computer revolution. While the machine audits were much more sophisticated and had better controls built in than the hand transcripts, they were no more than specialized adding machines.

While any discussion of the sophistication of the electronic audit would by necessity be outdated the moment it is written, the electronic audit has several advantages over the manual or machine audit that bear mentioning. Even with the machine audit, the job of tracing errors and proving the trial balance still fell on the auditor.

Today, however, computer systems have been designed to "think" in the sense that they can be programmed to search for the posting errors within the system, thus eliminating another need for the auditor to waste time. For example, a computer can be programmed to perform validity checks on accounts, meaning it can verify the accuracy of the postings. Essentially, the number of controls that can be programmed into the computer is unlimited.

Another advantage of the electronic system is that whatever information the auditor needs, as well as any number of reports management might want, can be arrayed in any fashion desired.

Perhaps the most important advantage of the electronic audit to the night auditor is that it allows more time to be spent on other activities. Most systems have commands that will allow the posting of room charges (room rate, room tax, and local telephone) to be done automatically. This in and of itself saves an enormous amount of time since the auditor does not have to post to every folio separately. There are many other ways in which these systems can save time. Perhaps the ultimate example is in the point-of-sale system, where the departmental charges are posted directly from the department cash register onto the guest folio, thus eliminating the need for the intermediary posting clerks.

For example, there are point-of-sale systems in lounges and dining rooms that will transmit any charge made at the location to the central computer, which will automatically post the charge to the indicated account. What these sophisticated systems demand is a different kind of auditor, one who understands the computer process and can perform the audit functions necessary in the electronic data-processing age. There are, of course, still problems associated with computer systems, including the one mentioned above concerning an overkill of reports generated. The problem also remains that accounts can be posted incorrectly. Many of the systems feature built-in safeguards that effectively minimize these human mistakes. One example is the point-of-sale register, which has prices programmed into it, so no pricing errors can be made.

A third problem concerns the fact that electronic machinery does not necessarily produce physical copies of the hotel's records. Thus, if the system should break down and no hard copies had been made, there might be no way to reproduce guest accounts. Worse, they might all be lost. It is extremely important that the operating procedure of the system prevent this catastrophic occurrence. It has happened that front office employees have had to literally knock on guest doors, find out if anyone is staying in the room, and then ask the guest how much his or her bill should be! There is one final caveat to all those who are learning computer, or even machine, night audit systems. Machines fail, and people who are responsible for generating the folios for presentation to the guest will always need to know how to do the job manually should the system go down. Even the most conscientious controller or front desk manager will inevitably face a crisis situation where the system cannot provide the information needed. It is for this reason all employees involved in the preparation of guest folios should know how to accumulate the required information necessary to keep open the flow between guest and hotel.

Hotel Purchasing

"Purchasing" is a term that has a variety of beverage facilities, to housekeeping, or to what meanings to different people. However, as it is generally used in the hospitality industry, it refers to the processes of buying: ascertaining need, locating and selecting suppliers, negotiating prices and terms, and ensuring adequate delivery. In addition, purchasing includes storage, receiving, incoming inspection, and capital goods procurement. Unfortunately for many managers in the hospitality industry, purchasing is often viewed as a supplementary staff activity that simply assures that hospitality organizations have an adequate supply of goods and services.

In fact, purchasing is a lot more than this. It is a key business activity that not only supports day-to-day operations but has a substantial impact on a variety of major business functions ranging from profit making to competitive positioning. The purpose of this article is to provide a broad overview of purchasing as a key business activity for hospitality operations.

Efficient operations

The enhancement of hospitality operations is probably purchasing's most basic contribution. It does this by ensuring that goods and services are purchased in the proper quantity at the proper quality, by making sure that deliveries are on time, and by managing storage in such a way that raw materials provide maximum service.

The department or managers charged with purchasing responsibility make this happen by working with operations managers to ascertain needs, by selecting reliable vendors, and by developing systems to assure a smooth throughput of raw goods in the operation-from the receiving dock to the storeroom, to the food and ever operating department requires these products.

Control

Purchasing exerts a significant influence on both quality and cost control. The quality of capital goods such as furniture, fixtures, and equipment (FF&E) affects both the image and the efficiency of an operation. Through product research and selection, purchasing managers assure that the proper FF&E items are available when they are needed. Similarly, the quality of raw food and beverage material is a key ingredient in the ultimate quality of finished goods. Managers charged with purchasing responsibility do a lot for food and beverage control by ensuring that purchased food and beverage items measure up to the quality specifications and by doing research to determine the necessary quality specifications for new items. Purchasing also exerts a major influence on cost control. For example, the cost of materials, including food, beverage, and supplies, often runs between 35 and 50 percent in food and beverage operations.

The potential for purchasers to save money through prudent and systematic buying is substantial. Hospitality organizations cannot be competitive unless they can deliver products and services to guests at a quality and a price that the guest feels is acceptable. When competition is based on price, as it often is, being able to purchase goods for resale at a lesser price than competitors goes a long way in enhancing competitive position.

Take, for example, a chain restaurant organization that is able to purchase prime ribs on a national contract basis that reduces their portion costs by 50 cents as compared to their competitors. A reduction of 50 cents in cost may mean that the restaurant has the ability to sell that item for as much as $1.25 less than their competitor. This improves their position vis-a-vis their competitors.

Profit

Purchasing influences profit in two very important ways. First, because every dollar saved through prudent and judicious purchasing goes directly toward the bottom line; and secondly, because the effective use of assets ultimately affects a firm's return on investment (ROI). Let's explore the relationship between purchasing savings and bottom-line results. This typical situation illustrates the profit-making potential of wise purchasing. Let's assume that the Sleep-AU-Night Hotel Company has a sales volume of approximately \$267 million, of which 30 percent, or approximately \$80 million, is contributed by food and beverage sales.

Material costs for food and beverage run about 40 percent on average, and pretax profit margins average around 10 percent, or about \$8 million. If management were astute and able to increase sales by \$20 million (25 percent), this would represent a \$2 million increase on the bottom line (0.10 x 20,000,000 = \$2,000,000). However, if purchasing were able to decrease the cost of sales to 37.5 percent, a 2.5 percent decrease, the \$2 million saved would go directly to the bottom line and thus equal as much on the bottom line as a 25 percent increase in sales! The following simple formula can be used to determine the sales equivalent of purchasing savings:

$$x = y \div z$$

Where:

x = the additional sales volume required to produce a pretax profit equal to that produced by a purchasing cost reduction

y = the reduction (expressed in dollars) in purchasing cost

z = the firm's pretax profit margin expressed as a decimal

In the preceding example, the equation would look like this:

$$x = \$2,000,000 - 0.10$$

$$x = \$20,000,000$$

Thus, it would require a \$20 million sales increase to equal the effect of a \$2 million cost reduction on the bottom line. While a 5 percent reduction in purchasing costs would be difficult, it is not impossible. Similarly, a 25 percent increase in sales would not be impossible, but it would be a lot more difficult than achieving a 5 percent reduction in costs. The effect of purchasing on ROA is similar, if less dramatic.

To assess an organization's overall performance, it is essential to consider the rate of return produced by all capital invested in the operation. This is called return on investment. While profit margin on sales is important, it is only half the ROI equation. The effective use of the organization's resources is equally important, and the formula for ROA is illustrates why. In accounting terms ROA is equal to the profit margin times the asset turnover rate.

In mathematical terms, this would be expressed as:

ROA = operating income (i.e., profit) ÷ total assets

ROA = (operating income - sales) × (sales - total assets)

As you can see, one half of the equation is devoted to how well managers use assets in relationship to total sales and the other is devoted to how well managers control costs in relationship to sales. Let's use the following example to illustrate: A hospitality organization has operating income of $1 million on $10 million in sales, and its total assets are equal to $9 million. If we plug this into the equation listed above for ROA, the equation would look like this:

($1,000,000 ÷ $10,000,000) × ($10,000,000 $9,000,000)

= 0.11, or 11% ROA

Purchasing can influence both the profit side through cost reduction and the asset side through total asset reduction. Let's say that through judicious purchasing we were able to increase operating income to $1.2 million and to decrease the asset base to $7 million. Let's calculate the effect on ROA:

($1,200,000 ÷ $10,000,000) × ($10,000,000 $7,000,000)
= 0.17, or 17% ROA

Thus the influence of purchasing on ROA is obvious.

The hotel purchasing function

The hotel purchasing function has not changed very much in the past 15 years. Up until the late 1980s various tax advantages were the primary reason for the construction of U.S. hotels. Providing a substantial return on investment was not expected or required. In our current economy, expectations on hotel profitability have changed. Profitability is now required along with maintaining the established level of quality. This has brought about a new interest in the purchasing function and greater importance placed on cost savings. Today, hotel managers realize that true cost savings generated in the purchasing department are dollars that drop directly to the bottom line

Without any associated incremental cost. It is not difficult to generate arbitrary savings; the true challenge is to create cost efficiency utilizing standard specification.

Purchasing for the hotel requires much more that obtaining three bids and circling the lowest price. The true definition of purchasing should be "purchasing the right product, at the right price, at the right time."

The statement sounds extremely simple, but when it is applied to the 1,000 to 2,000 items a hotel purchases, it presents a great challenge for the purchasing manager. The hotel purchasing function supports virtually every department within the property, whether purchasing chemicals for housekeeping or stewarding, office supplies for marketing, computer supplies for accounting, or food and beverage products for the restaurant outlets.

The purchasing manager usually reports to the hotel controller or to the hotel's financial control division.This will change in the future because there is a need for a more operational approach to managing the purchasing function. We need to build a team that is committed to the common goal of servicing our customers.

The reporting structure will begin to shift to operations, with the purchasing manager directly reporting to the general manager or to the executive assistant or operations manager in larger properties. This would help-to promote the philosophy of team building, and purchasing would support and service customers directly rather than acting as a support to other hotel departments.

With the increasing importance of the purchasing function, the utopian mission of the purchasing manager is to procure products and services cost effectively that will meet or exceed the customer's expectation. It is necessary to continually evaluate product specifications to incorporate new products and technology.

Purchasing organisation

The purchasing department can be organized into three basic areas:

— *Administrative*: This area would consist of pricing, vendor selection, and the purchase of nonstocked items. Nonstocked items are products purchased for immediate use or held in storage in other departments throughout the hotel.

— *Receiving*: There are two categories of receiving: (1) hotel goods, which are placed in storage in the purchasing area, or other items, Which are immediately issued to the requesting department, guest, or group; (2) items that have been shipped to a registered guest or expected guest or group.

— *Issuing*: Product issuing falls into two categories: (1) consumable food and beverage supplies, consisting of all food items and liquor, beer, wine, and mixes held in the purchasing department storerooms; (2) items such as office supplies, printed forms, and linen.

The staffing and segregation of duties vary from hotel to hotel, depending upon the property size and physical layout of the back-of-teh house areas.

Interdepartmental relationships

The purchasing manager develop close working relationships with key managers within the hotel. These relationships should build and demonstrate trust, confidence in judgment, and integrity. Key managers would include the following:

— Hotel general manager

— Executive assistant/operations managing

— Director of food and beverage

— Executive chef

— Director of housekeeping

Interaction between the purchasing manager and all other departments occurs on a regular basis. Verbal interaction is the most frequent either by telephone or in person. With the technological implementation of voice mail and electronic mail the communication process has become more efficient.

Most day-to-day interaction by the purchasing manager would involve some of the following key managers and issues:

— *General manager/executive assistant manager*: Issues relating to quality changes and all discussions regarding capital expenditure, food markets, quality, and availability information.

— *Director of food and beverage*: Unresolved food-purchasing issues and information related to wine, liquor, and beer purchases.

— *Executive chef*. Issues relating to food purchases. This area requires close communications regarding vendor performance, various size and physical layout of the back-of-the house areas.

— *Director of housekeeping*: Coordination and purchase of linens, paper goods (toilet paper, facial tissue, paper towels), uniforms, and laundry and cleaning chemicals.

A good purchasing manager bases purchasing decisions on the same criteria for all business decisions-data. No one can be an expert on every product available. This is where purchase specifications come into play. Written specifications must be developed for all key products. These products should also be tested periodically to verify that they meet or exceed specifications.

Purchasing sources

There are many sources of information for identifying producers, processors, and manufacturers. Technical data are also available. Suppliers are the best source of information.

The purchasing manager's day

7:00 AM. Inspect the quality of food and beverage consumables as they are delivered to the hotel. This includes rejecting incorrect or inferior products and then contacting the appropriate vendor(s) to rectify issues or determine another source, if necessary. The average daily purchase cost could vary from a low of $3,000 to a high of $50,000, depending on the size of the property and level of business.

9:00-11:00 AM. Attend daily meeting with the chef and the catering, stewarding, and banquet departments to review upcoming banquet business. Included would be a review of the room setup for each scheduled function, menus, and, most important, the guaranteed attendance numbers.

12:00 Noon. All food and beverage purchases have been received and issued. Inventory is now taken on all items in store to determine the next day's needs. After reviewing the current levels and calculating banquet business requirements, the vendors are selected. Orders are now placed with all suppliers. The number of suppliers could range from 1 to 25.

The rest of the afternoon is spent working on nonconsumable food and beverage purchases, obtaining bids, and following up on outstanding purchase orders overdue for delivery. The average work week for the purchasing manager is 50 to 60 hours and may include weekends. For the most part, normal business hours are usually 7:00 Am to 6:00 Pm, Monday through Friday, and 7:00 Am to noon on Saturday.

Cooperation and interaction

Corporate direction and control varies with each hotel company. As a rule, many hotel companies that manage rather than franchise their properties are more involved in setting policies and procedures. The corporate purchasing function is still viewed with some skepticism, although not as much as in the past. Today, purchasing is not a profit center and is established to benefit managed properties. The idea for the 1990s is to do more with less, and this applies to the corporate level as well as to the individual properties.

The most efficient method of purchasing system wide is targeting where dollars are spent and creating the most cost-efficient way to purchase high-volume items. Corporate hotel purchasing offices are currently working to accomplish this goal.

Hotel purchasing must focus on and utilize resources in the most efficient manner today. In the past, a heavy-handed approach was used to resolve issues with suppliers. As we move toward building partnerships with key vendors today, a teamwork approach provides an environment to build upon the strengths of both the hotel and the vendor. Another key component in business today is communication, both internal within the hotel and external with suppliers. One of our national Suppliers has the capability to link their customer service for placing orders with our domestic properties through a mainframe computer network linked to each property by PCs. Our hotels can place orders directly with the supplier through the network system and receive immediate confirmation. This nationwide system allows both our properties and the corporate office to access pricing, availability, and consumption.

Vital guidelines for property

While that was happening, more positive trends were evolving in hardware, software, and market scope. This article provides a summary of developments in each of those areas.

Hardware

During the past decade, the cost of computers and peripherals (in terms of performance per dollar invested) has dropped an average of more than 20 percent a year, and the trend is likely to continue. The hottest development of 1991 was the arrival of Intel's 486 microchip-An the PMS market. The 486 microprocessor doesn't fit all PMS situations, and not all the PMS packages can use it as a platform for their software.

However, the following real-world example shows what happens in a hotel situation where the 486 does fit:

— Early in 1992, a large, upscale Midwest hotel distributed specific bid specifications for a new PMS. Hardware requirements included 26 display screens and eight printers.

— Hardware cost of the lowest bid for a minicomputer-based system was $151,610. Lowest hardware bid for a LAN-based system was $169,427.

— When the hotel decided that both bids were beyond its budget, it asked the bidder of the UNIX-based minicomputer system to rebid the hardware using two interfaced micros with 386 chips. The hardware cost went down to $105,274.

— On behalf of the hotel, the bidder was later asked to reconfigure the hardware with a 486 based micro, which was then tested to be sure that capacity and response times were at least equal to the previous bids. The cost of the 486 based hardware configuration was $68,585. That is a remarkable difference.

The switch from mini-computer to two 386s, and then to a 486-based hardware configuration, resulted in a PMS installation that uses the same supplier's software at less than half the original hardware price. The continuing cost reduction in microcomputer hardware is very good for hotel budgets, but it is beginning to intrude on the market base of the major minicomputer and mainframe manufacturers. It's also actually hurting many of the PMS suppliers, because their revenue stream is dependent on a percentage of the' hardware price.

When hardware costs keep falling and the commission percentage remains the same, that means fewer revenue dollars for the PMS supplier. That downward trend in hardware prices is not likely to stop. For example, Intel is planning to introduce a 100-MHz version of its 486 chip in 1993, and its design engineers have already begun work on developing the next generation microchip. It will be a 64-bit reduced instruction set computing (RISC) microchip.

New software tools

For the properties it manages, Sheraton Corporation recently decided to standardize on the new UNIX-based PMS software developed by ECI Computer. It was then able to evaluate computer bids from several manufacturers before selecting Hewlett-Packard hardware for those properties. That portability wasn't always available, and that is one of the many key changes in software design that have been gaining importance during the past year. To understand the change in software tools, let's go back 20 years, when EECO (now ECI) pioneered the first successful PMS installation at the Dorado Beach Hotel in Puerto Rico.

The system was functional (but costly) and was based on proprietary components (hardware and software). Until the 1980s, any PMS developer had to decide which hardware would be used (Burroughs, DEC, Data General, Honeywell, IBM, NCR) and then develop the application using that hardware platform's proprietary operating system. As a result, the PMS developer was locked into specific (and limited) tools. In turn, the hotel's PMS was limited in growth and flexibility, and it could be run on only one brand of computer.

Lodgistix's first product used the &M Series/I. Computerized Lodging Systems chose MAI/ Basic Four. Encore Lodging Systems opted for DEC equipment. Hotel Information Systems developed the first PMS on the now long-defunct IBM System/32. EECO used a Data General processor as its base and manufactured the remaining hardware. The operating systems associated with those hardware choices had names like EDX, BOSS, TSC + RTH, SSP, and GCOS.

Other important new software tools are relational database management systems and fourth-generation languages. They have these advantages for the hotel PMS user:

— Software development, enhancement, and problem-solving time have been cut to less than half that needed with previous software tools. This means savings that can be passed on to the hotel in terms of competitive pricing and faster response to requests for software modification.

— In the past, if a change was made to a hotel PMS's data base, all the programs affected by the data base had to be recompiled.

For example, if the system had ten programs that used the reservations data base, all ten programs had to be modified and recompiled. This was time consuming and prone to errors. With today's program-development tools, the same scenario involves only one program change, and state-of-the-art software does all the rest.

Market scope

The classified pages of U.S. telephone directories list 73,068 hotels and motels; however, most of them were traditionally considered to be much too small to cost-justify a property management system. At the beginning of the 1980s, no more than 400 lodging properties could possibly install one, but the steady hardware cost reductions have kept increasing the size of the potential market.

Creating creativity

Creativity is the basis for improved customer service, new-customer acquisition, and a truly market-driven organization. Sales force creativity is that irrepressible energy that helps us improve on existing accounts and develop new ones. Creativity is the force that turns ordinary salespeople into account managers who are willing to develop strategic alliances with their clients. In contrast, the surefire signs of an unimaginative sales force that lacks creativity are repetition, strict adherence to company policy, and internal bickering.

Encourage and reward creativity

Do-it-by-the-book sales managers inevitably build mirror images in their sales force. Creativity enhancement begins with the leadership and vitality of management. Creativity within your sales group can be improved through a well-conceived and carefully administered program of behaviour modification. Frequent feedback and rewards for the accomplishment of tasks and objectives are textbook examples of positive reinforcement—and they work.

Outside stimuli

Artists, writers, and composers rely on their environmental and cultural experiences to stimulate creativity. Whether positive or negative, exciting or routine, outside influences can greatly affect creativity. Exposure to new stimuli can be generated by sales managers through a variety of inexpensive opportunities.

Keep Them Informed. Subscribe to periodicals such as trade magazines and professional publications. Encourage your salespeople to read these at home, during lunch breaks, or on the commuter train. Encourage discussion of interesting topics within these publications in formal sessions and informally during office discussions.

Give Them Culture. Purchase tickets from local theater, opera, or dance organizations and give them to members of your sales force for their personal use. Whenever possible, tie such gifts to the successful accomplishment of sales objectives. These small gifts probably aren't sufficient for rewarding sales performance, but they can be an excellent way to say "thanks" for tasks well done while exposing your people to the creative and performing arts.

Send Them Away. Develop a travel incentive program for high achievers. Hoteliers are in a unique position to benefit from virtually all travel, Combine a work-related assignment with the trip. Winners might be sent to a sister property in a resort area where they could meet that property's sales manager and members of the sales force. New friendships usually enhance a working vacation and provide new sales-related ideas.

Encourage Community Leadership. Encourage your staff to assume leadership positions in local organizations. It's surprising how much can be learned by organizing a Cub Scout pack or coaching Little League. Membership in the local school board, fraternal organizations, and other community groups helps break the couch potato syndrome and exposes one to new ideas.

Encourage Adult Education. Many companies offer tuition reimbursement for course work leading to a degree. Unfortunately, the end result too often is that the newly minted degree holder soon afterward undertakes a search for a new career. While this downside may be unavoidable, you can promote attendance at community colleges, technical schools, and other institutions that offer noncredit courses. Courses in creative writing, art history, and even auto mechanics can get the creative juices flowing. It all depends upon the individual.

Have Others Talk to Them. Invite interesting and provocative outsiders to your sales meetings or other group events. Motivational speakers may be included, but don't stack the deck with them. And don't restrict the topics that your guests may choose to cover. Speakers can cover a wide variety of subjects, from professional sales growth to community problems and economic development. Health professionals, travel and tourism experts, sales consultants, politicians, presidents of local banks, and university professors are a few of the kinds of speakers available in most communities.

Vary the Location of Your Sales Meetings. The sales force of many hotels rarely, if ever, ventures from the hotel for its own meetings. Occasionally hold your meetings in other, interesting places. For example, a tour boat operator on Virginia's James River hosts dozens of meetings that begin in Williamsburg and end at Norfolk, where guests can depart for the airport. Companies have found that the exhilaration of a boat ride and the changing scenery prime the creativity pump. Accompany meetings in off-site locations with a brief presentation of a topic related to that particular location.

Organize a Sales Blitz. A professionally managed sales blitz offers many advantages, including the spark to ignite individual creativity during a break in the routine of everyday sales activity.

In-house training and education

The education and training of hotel employees is a top priority for hotels that enjoy continuing success. A creative sales force is partially the result of consistent and creative in-house training and education.

Develop an Ongoing Program. In-house training and education are often the victims of fear or procrastination, especially when the sales manager feels unprepared to conduct or plan this function. In truth, no individual is in a better position to understand the needs of the sales force than the sales manager. Sales force training and education normally, don't call for the ongoing input of a trained educator. Consistency and regularity are dominant success factors. Try a variety of approaches. If one seems to be ineffective, change course—but offer the sales force some form of training and education on a regular basis.

Exchange Ideas, Problems, and Solutions. Involve your sales force in its own training and education. Don't rely on passive education to enhance creativity. The fact that peer-group study sessions are incorporated into nearly all multiday executive programs speaks well of their potential value when they are handled properly. But beware, unstructured and poorly planned group discussions often deteriorate into bull or gripe sessions.

Use Case Studies. These do not need to be complex business-school-type cases. Dozens of case studies are available within your own sales department. There you'll find cases in which sales opportunities were missed, important accounts were secured, unhappy customers were appeased, and many other scenarios.

Incorporate Education and Training into Sales Meetings. Require brief presentations during sales meetings by individual salespersons. Limit the time to 15 minutes to prevent a rambling and disruptive discourse. Expect those presentations to be accompanied by slides, overhead transparencies, or other visual aids. This practice serves as a useful training ground for customer presentations.

Encourage organized work habits

A myth persists that creativity is enhanced by disorganization and even an unkempt lifestyle. Perhaps that is true of a few individuals, but the creative achievements of modern architectural firms, advertising agencies, auto-design groups, engineering firms, and others provide contrary evidence.

Best-selling authors, famous sculptors, and other artists commonly report that their creations weren't born in a blaze of creativity but rather as the result of steady an organize work. An organized work schedule and a workplace free of unnecessary clutter and distractions need not be sterile or boring. One's work habits and work environment should be viewed as partners in a quest for enhanced creativity and increased sales productivity.

Participatory management

Salespeople far too often wait around for direction. Each member of the sales force must be actively involved in sales planning, which forces creative thinking. The sales manager's role is to facilitate that process. One way to do so is to use the Socratic approach of systematic questioning to force your salespeople into thinking their way through the process.

Additional ways to involve your sales staff in creative planning include the following:

Competitive Analysis. Examine carefully what it is your competition is *really* doing, and find out how well they're doing it. Such a study serves as an eye opener for staff and management, and thus provides a basis for creativity enhancement. ITT Sheraton Corporation refers to that process as "reverse engineering." Sheraton critically examines its competition through staff involvement and customer response collected via focus groups.

Account Analysis. If you sort your accounts by size of business and by demographic data, such as by zip code and type of business, you'll notice that important questions automatically emerge. For example: Why are some customers consistently key accounts when others in the same industry contribute little to occupancy and profit? Questions such as that are the natural product of account analysis. The ensuing discussion should lubricate even the most time-hardened wheels of thinking.

Sales Forecasts and Objectives. Never accept as the next period's projection of sales an estimate that is based simply on previous performance plus an addition for growth. Sales forecasts and objectives can be established only after a careful analysis of the external environment, competition, current accounts, and target customers.

Sales Strategies and Tactics. These are at the heart of any sales plan. This is where the action is, and where the chance for real creativity occurs. Encourage open discussion, brainstorming, and the freewheeling exchange of ideas.

Sales Budget. A sales manager can't be expected to deliver everything that the sales force desires, but an adequate budget allotment is more likely when supported by creative strategies that promise increased sales and higher yield.

Plan for career enrichment

Burnout is a hazard among those involved in hotel sales, as indicated by the high level of turnover at the property level. But if you track the movement of those salespeople, you'll find that many remain within the hospitality industry despite dissatisfaction with their previous position.

Burnout, it seems, is related to the property or specific job rather than dissatisfaction with the industry. Salespeople suffering from burnout are unlikely to be paragons of creativity. But a change in responsibilities and title may respark their enthusiasm and drive. Since upward or even lateral movement of a staff member is difficult to defend when that individual is in a slump, it's best to make such a move when the person is at her or his peak. This requires careful career-path planning for salespeople even if it means the creation of new positions. The temptation to leave top salespeople in their current position is a siren's call to impending disaster on burnout shoals. Creating new positions within the hotel sales department does not necessarily imply "empire building." Any hotel desiring an expanded customer base should consider the following.

Establish a Sales Position for Key or National Accounts. National account management and partnership marketing are becoming a way of life for business-to-business corporations. Viewed in its true perspective, that is precisely the definition of commercial hotels.

Establish an International Accounts Position. This is likely to be viewed as the prestige position within the sales department. Positions such as this (that is, positions to which your employees aspire) are desperately needed in hotel sales to overcome the otherwise flat nature of perceived advancement opportunities.

Create Other New Titles. Regroup accounts by industry type, geography, or other target market characteristics. Provide the encouragement and tools for salespeople to become experts in an industry or region.

Hotels located in areas with specific industrial concentrations such as computers, aircraft, food processing, textiles, or pulp and paper manufacturing might profit by training salespeople to become familiar with those industries. That may require attendance at regional trade shows, reading trade magazines, and gaining a working knowledge of that industry's key players. Offer your salespeople the opportunity to become industry-specific professionals, along with responsibility for developing a marketing and sales plan with budget recommendations. Then watch to see if creativity doesn't improve.

Provide Transfer opportunities to Sister Properties. Creativity and enthusiasm often drop for personal reasons that have no cause within the organization. Rather than lose those individuals to the marketplace, assist them by arranging a transfer to a sister property. Consider their tenure with you as professional training, and keep your door open for those salespeople who may be headed in your direction from other properties in your chain.

Plan for a Career Path. Include your salespeople in career-path planning. Avoidance of this critical managerial responsibility inevitably leads to employee frustration and burnout—and too often to feelings of hopelessness. Many salespeople require frequent reinforcement concerning their career paths and must regularly be convinced that they haven't been overlooked.

Paving the way

Magic bullets that enhance and maintain sales force creativity are a myth. This warning is clearly voiced by Michael B. Peceri, president of Marquis Hotels and Resorts. "When a sales force becomes complacent, I look for ways to motivate it, but I would be hard-pressed to find a way to take a complacent sales force and make it creative." The road to improved creativity is paved with basic management skills. Creativity enhancement is not a distinct problem requiring a unique management response but is instead an ongoing function of management and the basis for solid and continuing growth in an increasingly competitive environment.

Time palnning

The purpose of time planning for sales is to assist members of the sales force to establish priorities, to meet objectives, and to be efficient and content. Stress, common among hotel salespeople, is counterproductive to any property's objectives. By planning your sales priorities within a schedule, stress can be reduced. Salespeople who realize late in the sales period that their quotas are unlikely to be met are candidates for high levels of stress and poor performance.

True sales success in the hotel industry never results from a few large accounts signed at the last minute. Instead, sales achievement is the result of continuous and steady effort throughout the year. Unfortunately, far too many salespeople fail to use their time effectively and therefore suffer in their sales performance. For example, it's common to see hotel salespeople devoting one or more mornings each week to such paperwork as completing expense or call reports.

Annual time plans

The process of time planning forces one to consider how the various tasks necessary to achieve success can best be accomplished within a limited time frame. Time plans for the entire year are not expected to describe how each week or day will be used but, rather, to identify the major tasks to be performed during the year and their relative allocation by month. Used correctly, an annual time plan assists salespeople to form the big picture concerning what is needed to meet and exceed objectives.

Annual time plans must never be enforced as binding contracts, but instead should be viewed as aides to enhance personal performance. The annual time plan is to be completed once each year and should be incorporated into your annual sales planning process. The basis for any sales plan is the identification of key and marginal accounts accompanied by new target account prospects and estimates of sales volume from each. Strategies and tactics to retain old accounts and add new ones provide the basis for estimating the amount of time necessary to accomplish the primary tasks.

Weekly time plans

Weekly sales plans must be completed prior to Monday morning. Beware of delaying weekly planning until the start of the weekend, however, when it may hang like the sword of Damocles over the head of the salesperson. In such cases, the task of weekly sales planning takes on an ominous tone far in excess of its actual level of difficulty. The assistance of an experienced sales manager in the development of weekly plans is often the difference between a frustrating and wasted week or genuine sales progress. Veteran salespeople may need little assistance but new salespeople can generally always benefit. Review the weekly plans of salespeople and look for these major time traps:

— Uneven daily workloads.

— Over or underestimation of daily sales calls.

— Widespread geographical dispersion of sales calls.

— Little or no time for sales administration tasks.

— Overemphasis on new account prospecting with little time allocated for existing account followup.

Daily time plans

No aspect of time planning is more important than the daily plan: Annual sales success is nothing more than the accumulation of successful sales days. An award-winning salesperson was asked what contributed to his sales success. The reply was simple: "I plan the activities of each day the night before. Many other salespeople in this company don't begin to plan until they are behind the wheel of their car."

Sales success is truly the result of planning each day to maximize sales effectiveness while minimizing travel and nonessential tasks. All sales managers must continuously teach and reinforce this basic concept. Establish objectives for each appointment: Forget the notion that sales calls should be made "just to stay in touch." Decision makers simply don't have the time for appointments that serve no purpose. But they will take the time to learn about new products and benefits, to hear how to solve a service problem, to listen to cost-savings ideas, and to meet with salespeople who can assist them in the performance of their job.

The advent of integrated, computerized record keeping has the potential to demonstrate variances in sales performance among individual members of the sales force. Those salespeople well grounded in the use of time planning have little to fear from this or other technology-based management tools.

While many of these suggestions for time management may seem like common sense, it is true that, as the saying goes, common sense is not that common. If you combine the practical approach to time management with the creative approach to generating sales, your hotel will benefit from an efficient, motivated, and productive sales staff.

Yield management

When measuring sales performance, hotel management can march to many drummers. Some managements heed the beat of occupancy, others watch the average rate, and still others compare actual results to budget. Management's selection of performance criteria affects the decision-making, priority-setting, and overall behaviour of all departments and units within a hotel company. Many of the traditional performance criteria employed by the industry today do not foster decisions that are in the best interest of the hotel.

The sales department, measured by room-night productivity, for instance, will inevitably accept group business whenever possible—and then be forced to turn away higher-paying, later-booking individual customers. In this chapter we will explain how an integrated measurement technique, yield management, can help a hotel gain an optimum business mix and meet its revenue goals. Reduced to essentials, hotels are in the business of generating revenue from space. Guest rooms, restaurant seats, and function rooms are the scarce resource of hotels, in much the same way that seats are the scarce resource of the airline industry.

Percentage

The basic yield statistic is a straightforward measure of the effectiveness of practices and policies applied to generating revenue from room sales. This statistic can be expressed as follows:

$$\text{Yield} = \frac{\text{Revenue Realized}}{\text{Revenue Potential}}$$

Revenue potential is the income that could be secured if 100 percent of available rooms are sold at their *full rack rates*. So, for a 300-room hotel with a $100 rack rate, the revenue potential is $30,000. Revenue realized is the actual sales receipts. If the hotel sold 200 rooms at an average rate of $80, the revenue realized would be $16,000. The yield would be $16,000 divided by $30,000, or 53.3 percent.

Many combinations of occupancy and average rate could result in the same revenue and the same yield percentage, as shown in Exhibit 1. Some readers might contend that all the cases of a 53.3 percent yield are not equal. One could assert that Case A is preferable, for instance, because the cost of cleaning and heating 160 rooms is lower than any of the alternatives.

Someone else might say that having 300 occupied rooms is best, because a full house would inevitably mean more revenues in other profit centers, such as restaurants, lounges, and telephones. The reader sensitive to how statistics can create powerful impressions might hold that one of the intermediate alternatives was best, because it would be least likely to raise a red flag with the owners or at headquarters.

In fact, each of the foregoing arguments has validity. All combinations of rate and room sales that produce the same yield are equally desirable to the hotel.

Exhibit 1
Different scenarios for identical revenues

Case	Rooms Sold	Occupancy	Average Rate	Rooms Revenue	Yield(%)
A	160	53.3%	$100.00	$16,000	53.3%
B	180	60.0	88.88	16,000	53.3
C	220	73.3	72.72	16,000	53.3
D	240	80.0	66.66	16,000	53.3
E	260	86.6	61.53	16,000	53.3
F	280	93.3	57.14	16,000	53.3
G	300	100.0	53.33	16,000	53.3

Close cousins

The yield statistic is closely related to the industry standbys of occupancy percentage and average rate. The occupancy percentage, of course, is actually a ratio of the number of rooms sold to the rooms available for sale. We usually express average rate as a simple dollar figure, but we could also express the average rate as a ratio of actual rate to potential rate. In Case B, for instance, the average rate ratio is $88.88 divided by $100, or about 89 percent. Knowing that you have an 89 percent rate ratio and a 60 percent occupancy rate is not especially helpful, until you multiply the ratios together. So the yield statistic is closely related to the combination of occupancy and average rate. The only difference is that average rate is converted into a ratio.

Seesaw

Most seasoned managers know that results like case B would likely occasion a call from headquarters or owners asking why occupancy was so low. In response to this concern, management might relax rate expectations regarding groups, sell more rooms to economy-minded transients, and allocate more rooms for specially priced packages. If these measures are effective, the results for the next month might look more like Case E, in which occupancy rises while average rate sinks. The manager then would not be surprised to receive another call, this one inquiring why average rate was so low. The point here is that both cases are essentially equal in terms of revenue and yield, and they are probably equally profitable for the hotel. By considering yield, the manager would have a single, integrated measure that tracks closely with contribution to profitability. Hilton Hotels Corporation takes this approach. Hilton's director of marketing said, "Yield is the key word around Hilton. Concerns with average rate and occupancy have been replaced with yield and revenue."

Boosting yield

Management's responsibility is to increase yield. There are two basic yield-management strategies, each appropriate for different conditions of guest room supply and demand. High demand calls for tactics geared to maximizing the revenue associated with rooms sold (high rates). Excess supply requires an emphasis on maximum room sales, even if a lower average rate is the cost associated with these tactics.

A hotel's effectiveness in improving yield is based on its infrastructure in the following four critical areas:

1. *Forecasting:* Good forecasts of daily rooms demand with a system for continuous updating.
2. *Systems and procedures:* Automated systems, rate-setting policies, promotional packaging, and specially trained personnel, with sufficient flexibility to adapt to changes in demand conditions.
3. *Strategic and tactical plans:* Cohesive strategies supported by tactics that can quickly respond to varying demand conditions.
4. *Feedback systems:* Methods to assess the effectiveness of tactics and provide information vital to personnel seeking to improve performance.

Forecasting

The most effective yield-management tactics have a daily, rather than seasonal, orientation. For example, decisions regarding the availability of packages designed for rate-sensitive markets should be made for individual future days, and not as a single policy for all days in a season. Forecasting must provide estimates of future demand on a daily basis for it to be helpful in optimizing yield. Many hotels that make daily forecasts look only at the upcoming 60 to 90 days. Since most commercial hotels realize the vast majority of transient reservations within a few weeks of receiving them, daily forecasts with a two- or three-month horizon would seem sufficient. But longer-range estimates of transient demand are critical for hotels that do even a small portion of their business with group segments.

The tradeoff between group business and transient business is often one of occupancy versus rate.

Groups generally make room commitments far in advance of transients, thereby boosting known occupancy percentages. But most hotels find that transient guests, on average, pay higher rates than do groups. Therefore, the displacement of future, high-rate transient reservations by groups that are paying lower rates must be a carefully considered decision.

This decision takes on an added dimension when one considers that a portion of the displaced transients will be spending the night at a competitor's hotel. It is clearly imperative to base today's decision on whether to book a prospective group on forecasted transient demand for the specific days under consideration.

The common shorthand approach of considering all Mondays through Thursdays as essentially the same often leads to unwise displacement or to empty rooms that could have been filled.

Forecasts must consider both transient and group demand. In evaluating whether to book a group two years in advance at a marginal rate, the sales manager must determine the likelihood of displacing other groups, as yet unknown to the hotel, that might be willing to pay higher rates. Computer-assisted forecasting methods can facilitate the necessary data handling and analyses. The risk inherent in some forecasting models is their oversimplification of the factors affecting demand. A program that fails to look at the interaction between neighbouring days, for example, may result in misinformation. Taking each day individually, a program might predict occupancy well in excess of 100 percent on Monday night and 95 percent on Tuesday night. A well-thought-out program would make adjustments; in the Tuesday estimate to reflect the lack of availability on Monday. If Monday sells out prematurely, Tuesday's full potential will not be realized.

Systems and procedures

Daily demand forecasts, regardless of accuracy, are not sufficient to enhance yield. Policies, procedures, and personnel trained for yield maximization must be in place to take advantage of the forecasts and act in ways that enhance the property's revenues. The following is sampling of tactics that cultivate higher yields.

High demand

When demand is high, a hotel can (1) restrict or close availability of low-rate categories and packages to transients, (2) require minimum lengths of stay, and (3) commit rooms only to those groups willing to pay higher rates.

Low demand

When demand is low, a hotel can (1) provide reservation agents with special promotional rates to offer transients who balk at standard rates, (2) solicit group business from organizations and segments that are characteristically rate-sensitive, and (3) promote limited-availability low-cost packages to the local market. Though these tactics are not novel, their application in many busy hotels is often less than thorough.

Sometimes the intention is right, but the tactic is off-target. Until recently, a major hotel company had a policy of closing lower rates on a fixed schedule, according to the number of rooms left to sell. This meant that someone calling for a reservation when there were 300 unsold rooms would be quoted lower rates than another caller inquiring about the same date when only 100 rooms remained. This method considered neither the time left to sell the remaining rooms nor estimates of the potential, unrealized demand. In many cases, the inflexibility of computer systems hampers yield-management efforts.

Most central reservation systems, when providing rates to reservation agents in response to an inquiry, display the rates that are available on the arrival date requested. But demand on the arrival date will not, in many cases, be representative of demand during the entire length of stay. The following example illustrates this point. Say that a reservation agent's computer is programmed to show the following rates on given days of the week.

	Available Rates				
Sunday	110	95	85	75	65
Monday	110	95			
Tuesday	110				
Wednesday	110	95	85	75	65
Thursday	110	95	85	75	65

Case A. A caller inquiring about a three-day stay beginning on Sunday could be quoted five rates, all the way down to $65. These rate quotes would undermine efforts to maximize yield, given that both Monday and Tuesday are high-demand days.

Case B. A caller inquiring about a three-day stay beginning on Tuesday would be quoted only one rate, $110. Such rate inflexibility would increase the likelihood that the caller would shop around for lower rates. Given that Wednesday and Thursday are low-demand days, the loss of this reservation would be unfortunate. Other central reservation systems take a different approach. They display only those rates that are available for all the days requested. Using the examples above, only $110 would be quoted in both cases. Such an approach would be unjustifiably restrictive if yield maximization is the objective.

Often it is not an automated system that confounds full implementation of yield-management tactics, but the approaches taken to training personnel and monitoring their performance. For example, a sales manager's productivity is often measured in terms of the number of room-nights booked. The implicit assumption in this approach is that all room-nights are equally beneficial to the hotel, regardless of rate.

Many companies refine this crierion by looking at monthly sales manager totals of both room-nights and average rate. Though this approach provides more data, it does not necessarily shed light on the real impact of each sales manager's bookings. The chart in Exhibit 3 helps to demonstrate the problem. All four sales managers in the example booked 600 room-nights at an average rate of $100. Does that mean they all did an equally good job in contributing to the hotel's yield? A case can be made for ranking the sales managers in the following way.

— Sales manager D: all bookings on low-demand days.

— Sales manager A: relatively few high-demand days.

— Sales manager B: high proportion of high-demand days booked, high likelihood of transient displacement.

— Sales manager C: high proportion of high-demand days, many sold at a relatively low rate.

The difference in the contribution made by sales managers D and C is substantial. When traditional measures of productivity are unable to demonstrate this difference statistically, there is little motivation for sales managers to adapt their behaviour to maximize contribution.

A sales manager faced with a large, rate-sensitive group eager to book low-demand days might think twice before taking the group if it would substantially lower the average rate of all his bookings for the month. Any measure that creates such a conflict between the hotel's best interest and the statistical representation of productivity is seriously flawed and will not effectively promote yield maximization.

Boykin Management Company, based in Cleveland, has instituted a sales incentive system that rewards those efforts of sales managers that contribute to realization of an optimum business mix. Hyatt Hotels is testing an incentive system that gives salespeople varying credit, depending on market demand factors. Bookings into low-demand days accrue more points than those into days with high or excess demand. To be assured of systems and procedures that encourage yield maximization, that purpose must be designed specifically into the system. Rarely will the traditional approaches coincidentally promote supportive decision making and behaviour. Fortunately, conscientious employees often attempt to compensate for the limitations they find in a hotel's systems and procedures.

Strategy and tactics

Appropriate planning is integral to yield management. Often planning takes the shape of "last year's results plus 10 percent," followed by a list of tasks to achieve the new target. Planning for maximum yield takes a different approach. It asks questions like "What would be our mix of market segments if we were to maximize yield?" Too often the segment mix that made good business sense a few years ago is perpetuated simply because this question has not been asked.

Many critical decisions are made by a casual continuation of past practices, rather than an analysis of and choice for the future. Examples of such inertia include commitments to base accounts (e.g., crew rooms), levels of participation in citywide conventions, discounted rates for local organizations that have the potential to produce a certain volume of business, and a desired ratio of transient to group room-nights.

Military planners draft tactical blueprints to take advantage of any battlefield condition that might arise. Though a hotel's competitive and market environments do not have the same level of complexity or consequence, the importance of thoughtful and integrated plans is still fundamental.

In most hotels, the responsibility for responding to market conditions is distributed among many departments, often resulting in actions with little chance of maximizing yield and with significant potential for fostering disharmony between departments.

Hotels managed by Boykin carefully prepare optimum business-mix scenarios, specifying what size and types of group and catering business should be on the books, and by when. If the proposed optimum mix is not achieved by a certain time, say 12 months prior to a future week, a mid-term optimum scenario is activated to guide sales efforts and decision making. Both long- and mid-term plans are guided by the demand and value from transient segments.

Front desk, reservations, and sales departments all play a consequential role in yield-related decisions. Their views of the world, however, are often not unlike the people who had to describe the elephant based only on their sense of touch.

One felt the elephant as a tree trunk, one as a rope,

one as a hose, one as a dagger, and one as a solid wall. Each was right, of course, but none was in touch with the whole story. A proper tactical plan has all of its decision making oriented toward the same goal of yield maximization. Departments work in concert supported by actions and decision rules appropriate for current and forecast market conditions.

As a result, negotiations with prospective groups, rate quotations to inquiring transients, and determination of package availabilities all coordinate and contribute to optimization of yield.

Both Hyatt and Hilton report better inter-departmental working relationships since instituting yield-management systems. The director of sales and marketing information for Hyatt stated: "Communications between sales and reservations have increased dramatically."

Even when a hotel has drafted an effective tactical plan, implementation soon becomes unwieldy. Short- and long-term forecasts must be kept up to date amid changing commitments to groups (e.g., bookings, cancellations, and block changes), varying behaviour of volume and base accounts, shifting -availability of competitive properties, and the continuous flow of local and national events influencing transient demand.

Data and forecasts must be kept up to date for as far into the future as the hotel is likely to book groups. Couple these difficulties with the variety of tactics that must go into play as the prognosis for the future evolves, and one begins to see how overwhelming the job can become. Furthermore, many seemingly simple tactics are often far more complex once explored. For example, one yield-maximizing tactic is to analyse the tradeoff between the value of a prospective group and the loss associated with the probable displacement of transient business. An example will highlight the complexities hidden beneath a seemingly simple solution.

Feedback

Systematic feedback is needed to assess the effectiveness of forecasts, the impact of tactics, and the performance of individuals and departments in their efforts to raise the hotel's yield. Much of the data that should be tracked are similar to numbers already gathered by many, hotels, while some of the data are fundamentally different. A simple example will demonstrate the importance of often overlooked information. There are a variety of methods and models for forecasting transient demand. All would gain enhanced accuracy if complete data were available on transient requests that were lost or turned down and why they were not accommodated. Most reservations systems give agents the opportunity to enter lost business, but most do not have a systematic way to ensure that all lost business and related dates are recorded. In forecasting models, partial data can mislead or camouflage important trends.

Personnel tend to focus their efforts on ways that will have the greatest impact on the measures by which their performance is assessed. Regular feedback can encourage yield-oriented behaviour and decision making. As an example, both individual hotels and large central reservation centers have difficulty determining agent effectiveness. They often resort to ancillary measures such as average call duration or completed calls per hour. A yield-oriented approach compares the revenue associated with an agent's actual bookings to the potential associated with all calls taken by the agent. Such an approach encourages bookings at higher average rates, without discouraging lower rates when appropriate. This ratio is not sufficient in itself to assess agent effectiveness, but it does keep agents continuously attending to yield.

Feedback on the effect of tactics can lead to optimization of their application. Reservations managers continuously open and restrict the availability of certain rate categories in the hope of neither underselling a room nor having a room that could have been sold go empty. Their task is to balance the superior revenues associated with higher rate quotations against the greater likelihood of a conversion, or booking, if lower rates are offered.

A system with data on the conversion factor associated with different rate-quotation schemes, room availability, and estimates of demand can automatically select the rate-quotation approach with the greatest potential. Regular and germane feedback provides encouragement, sets priorities, and enables the use of yield-management techniques that otherwise would be impossible.

Hotel companies adopting yield-management systems and techniques have achieved good results.

— Reservations for Hyatt's Regency Club concierge floors have climbed by 20 percent, and the average rate for all reservations from its central reservation center has increased since yield management has been instituted.

— Diligent forecasting and yield-oriented planning has enhanced Hyatt's successful Gold Passport frequent traveller program by ensuring sufficient room availability to accommodate demand.

— Many Hilton hotels have set all-time revenue records. One property experienced a $7.50 increase in transient average rate with no reduction in occupancy the first month after installing a yield-management system.

Hotels marching to the drumbeat of yield optimization discover organizational benefits as well as improvements on the bottom line. Interdepartmental conflicts diminish as traditional performance measures are replaced by criteria that integrate efforts across departmental lines. Clear plans and relevant criteria allow decision making to move downward within the organization, leading to greater efficiency and heightened job satisfaction.

Many yield-management methods are made practical by the advent of affordable computing power. The practices of the past, in many cases, reflect the available technology of those times.

New capabilities have engendered fresh thinking and call for a fundamental reconceptualization of the scope of traditional computer applications in the hotel industry. The practices, policies, and systems that contribute to yield management share a common orientation—namely, maximum return on a scarce resource (hotel rooms). The same approach has been applied in -modified formats to optimizing returns on function space and food and beverage facilities.

Yield management is not merely an adjunct to traditional managerial approaches. Instead, it represents a fundamental basis for concentrating organizational efforts. Yet it is not such a radical departure from established approaches as to force a disruptive transition. Though in many ways the age of yield orientation is just dawning, and some early experiences will be less than fully successful, the promise of this technique is of such magnitude that it demands immediate attention.

Hotel promotions

Fierce competition abounds, extreme market segmentation is prevalent, and occupancy levels and profits are down throughout the hotel industry. As a partial response to these problems, the hotel industry has made significant changes in methods used to quote room prices and in the sale of its rooms through central or local reservation systems. To maximize revenue, many hotels have implemented yield-management systems that adjust "room rates in response to the level of rooms booked for future arrival dates".

Computer systems, sales incentive programs, and the retraining of reservation personnel and others are necessary in order to produce "the best possible return, or yield, from the space available".

While the hotel management it attempting to boost revenues, they may be simultaneously and actively promoting discount programs to attract weekend guests, senior citizens, corporate accounts, government contracts, and families. Potential guests often respond to advertisements for reduced-rate rooms and discount packages by calling the hotel reservation system.

Quoting prices

Some focus on hotel actions and policy and look only at the effectiveness of marketing programs, not their legality. The same methods, practices, and policies that have been considered ineffective or questionable marketing practices may also be violations of unfair and deceptive acts and practices statutes. Managers, personnel, and agents may intentionally ignore corporate policy. Attaining corporate, department, or personal revenue goals in order to maximize their own evaluations or compensation might be reasons these people ignore policy. They may also unknowingly fail to provide information, or they may provide incorrect information.

Another study by Lewis also found that customers calling for information about the availability of rooms or about advertised prices are frequently given erroneous information. "When queried about these low rates in random phone calls to their 800 number reservation desk, these firms all said their rooms were sold out. We can only assume that, very suddenly, 67 percent of these chain hotels are full on weekends." The reservation clerk is telling the customer that the room is sold out, when clearly the room is available, but not at that price.

Systems exist today that may prevent customers from obtaining available rooms at advertised prices. In addition, the advertised price information may be either unavailable to the reservation personnel or very difficult to access. Lewis and Roan recount a story in which a prospective customer called a hotel and attempted to reserve a room at an advertised discount rate. The reservation clerk, who used a computer, consistently rebuffed the caller from obtaining information as to the availability of a room at the advertised price.

Were there any rooms available at the stated price? Was there any limitation stated in the advertisement as to the supply of rooms and/or availability only at certain locations? It is difficult to determine in this case if the clerk is using yield-management techniques or if the computer is really preventing the clerk from providing requested information.

This activity is an example of a bait and switch that is probably a violation of the unfair and deceptive acts and practices statutes of federal and most state laws. This hotel and others that operate in this manner are clearly placing themselves at risk of a class-action suit that would demand triple damages and attorneys' fees. If one could prove that other prospective customers were treated in the same manner, or that it was corporate policy to provide room and price information in this manner, the hotel chain and hotel management could be in for a very costly and embarrassing lawsuit.

Unfair and deceptive acts and practices

The Federal Trade Commission (FTC) Act declares that "unfair and deceptive acts and practices in or affecting commerce, are declared unlawful." According to the National Consumer Law Center, all 50 U.S. states and the District of Columbia have passed "little FTC legislation that applies to most consumer transactions, and is aimed at preventing consumer deception and abuse in the marketplace." Federal and state unfair and deceptive acts and practices statutes are intended to be broad and flexible so that almost any type of abusive business practice can be considered to be unfair and/or deceptive. These business practices are generally classified under the following groups of behaviour:

1. Deception or statutory fraud
2. Unconscionability
3. Unsubstantiated claims
4. General misrepresentation
5. High-pressure or coercive sales techniques
6. Deceptive performance practices
7. Deceptive practice inducements
8. Unfairness

Deceptive practices

To prove that a practice is deceptive, one must show that it has a tendency or capacity to deceive only a minority of consumers; as detailed in *FTC v. Colgate Palmolive Company*. It is important to understand that it is not necessary that a hotel or business intends to deceive the customer. An act can be "deceptive" even if the perpetrator did not intend to deceive. In 1984 the FTC promulgated standards to be used in determining whether a practice should be considered deceptive. Bailey and Pertschuk state that a practice is deceptive if:

1. The practice is likely to mislead consumers.
2. A consumer is deceived while behaving reasonably in the circumstances.
3. The deception is material to the consumer, that is, the consumer would have acted differently if not for the deceptive practice.

Actual deception need not be proved, but only that the practice had the capacity to deceive. In addition, *FTC v. Colgate Palmolive Company* stated that a practice is deceptive if it will affect a substantial number of consumers and will cause consumers to act differently from how they would have acted if the deceptive practice had not been used.

Unfair practices

Unfair practices are easier to prove than deceptive practices because the standards required to prove deception generally require a finding of a more onerous activity. In the Supreme Court case, *FTC v. Sperry and Hutchinson Company,* the Court created standards for practices that were to be considered unfair, even if the practice was not deceptive. The Court said that unfairness would be determined by the following factors:

1. Whether the practice, without necessarily having been previously considered unlawful, offends public policy... whether it is within at least the penumbra of some common law, statutory, or other established concept of unfairness;
2. Whether the practice is immoral, unethical, oppressive, or unscrupulous;
3. Whether the practice causes substantial injury to consumers.

In language that could apply to hotels and their pricing and reservation practices, the Supreme Court also states:

> [the] wide variety of decisions interpreting the elusive concept of unfairness at least makes clear that a method of selling violates section 5 [of the Federal Trade Commission Act] if it is exploitive or inequitable, and if, in addition to being morally objectionable, it is seriously detrimental to consumers or others.

Violations of the Federal Trade Commission Act do not allow individuals who may have been the victims of unfair or deceptive acts and practices the right to a private remedy for damages or for injunctive relief. That is, the individual is not empowered to seek legal remedies or damages. Rather, the FTC is granted sole authority to enforce the Federal Trade Commission Act according to U.S.C. sec. 45 (a).

To prevent misconduct and to encourage lawsuits by individuals, the unfair and deceptive acts and practices laws of most states provide for private damage claims. Individuals who have been wronged can sue on their own behalf. These statues include such "private remedies as attorneys' fees for prevailing consumers and punitive, treble or minimum damage awards". In addition, most state statutes allow class-action suits against those accused of unfair or deceptive acts and practices. In many situations where a consumer has been wronged, the amount of the actual damages sustained may not be large enough to cause the injured customer to hire a lawyer to sue.

The class-action suit allows customers to sue on behalf of the entire class of customers who have been injured in a similar way, and to have their attorney collect their legal fees from the party being sued. The class-action lawsuit is a very powerful tool that can be effectively used to encourage consumers and their attorneys to turn a seemingly insignificant claim into one with the potential for a tremendous damage award.

Bait and switch

One practice that has been specifically recognized as a deceptive practice pursuant to the unfair and deceptive acts and practices statutes is what is referred to as a "bait and switch."

A customer is baited or lured by an advertisement that offers a particular product or service at an attractive price. When the customer responds to the advertisement, the salesperson switches the customer to a higher-priced product. The deception occurs because the seller never had any intention of selling the advertised item, but meant to use the low price to get people to come to the store".

The Federal Trade Commission states:

> No act or practice should be engaged in by an advertiser to discourage the purchase of the advertised merchandise as part of a bait scheme to sell other merchandise. Some of the acts or practices which will be considered to be part of a bait and switch scheme are:
>
> a. The refusal to show, demonstrate, or sell the product offered in accordance with the terms of the offer,
>
> b. The disparagement by acts or words of the advertised product,
>
> c. The failure to have available at all outlets listed in the advertisement a sufficient quantity of the advertised product to meet reasonably anticipated demands, unless the advertisement clearly and adequately discloses that the supply is limited and/ or the merchandise is available only at designated outlets,

d. The refusal to take orders for the advertised merchandise,

e. Use of a sales plan or method of compensation for sales [persons], designed to prevent or discourage them selling the advertised product.

Reservation systems should be designed that "would provide the reservation agent with a suggested sequence of quotations that would lead to maximum profitability". Could the computer be programmed in such a way so that reservation clerks are not even aware of advertised rates and packages? Without some specific guidelines, it is easy to see how a management company, manager, computer programmer, or even a reservation clerk could get carried away and participate, knowingly or unknowingly, in illegal activities.

The airlines use yield management, so it must be legal

When confronted with information that certain yield-management activities or reservation practices may be violations of state or federal unfair and deceptive acts and practices, many people within the hospitality industry respond that it is only doing what the airline industry has done very successfully for years. The *Wall Street Journal* has noted:

Much to fliers' dismay, airlines often promote bargain fares that aren't available on all flights. Such ads "fit the classic bait and switch," says Albert Sheldon, Deputy Attorney General of the State of California. While the Federal Trade Commission has taken a laissez-faire attitude toward numerous pricing activities by the airlines, many states have attempted to restrain airline pricing and reservation activity with the enforcement of their unfair and deceptive acts and practices statutes.

The hotel industry is not free to emulate the actions of the airline industry when it operates yield-management systems. The airline industry cannot be prosecuted for a practice that is considered to be unfair and deceptive under state law, whereas the hotel industry may be prosecuted for the same practice.

Avoiding unfair and deceptive acts and practices

In the rush to implement yield-management systems, valid concerns over the legality of such implementation be easily overlooked or disregarded. One of the goals of this chapter is to provide some guidance to those responsible for the implementation of yield-management systems, so that they can maximize revenues in a legal manner.

Some simple steps can be taken so that your management company, hotel chain, employees, shareholders, and investors are not placed in an unwanted, costly, embarrassing, and illegal situation. In addition, consultation with counsel is advised to ensure that your specific actions are legal. The following are some basic steps to take:

1. All advertisements should "clearly and adequately disclose that supply is limited and/or the merchandise is available at designated outlets".

The FTC allows the advertising of discounts for products that have limited availability, but only if that limited availability is stated in the advertisements. Note that the advertisement (and not the reservation clerk) must indicate that the supply is limited. If the advertisement does not specify that there is limited supply or that it is available only at designated outlets, then it is the responsibility of the hotel to provide "a sufficient quantity of the advertised product to meet reasonably anticipated demands".

2. Integrate your marketing efforts and reservation practices. Involve marketing and advertising people

with your plans and strategies to ensure that the above requirements are met.

3. Quote the advertised rate first. If a customer calls and inquires about a special promotion or rate, then that customer should be immediately provided with pricing and availability information for that particular package. Attempts to start quoting to that customer at higher rates or at rack rates to discourage or to disparage that package should be avoided.
4. Train all employees to be aware of unfair and deceptive acts and practices regulations. Sensitize them to the subtle and not so subtle differences between legal and illegal behaviour. Encourage them to question practices that are unethical, immoral, and unscrupulous. Training sessions with managers and legal counsel may be helpful.
5. Have your technology work in a legal, rather than illegal, manner. Demand that your systems engineers he familiar with legal requirements. Require from your system that if a customer asks about an advertised price or package the system will allow the reservation personnel to immediately access the information and book the room at the advertised price.
6. Avoid sales incentive compensation plans that may cause reservation agents or personnel and managers to become too aggressive in their pursuit of higher yields. Avoid plans that discourage employees from selling the advertised lower-priced rooms and packages. Avoid compensation plans that do not pay commissions on the lower-priced rooms but only on the higher-priced rooms. When customers respond to advertisements for lower-priced rooms, it is extremely, easy for clerks or managers who are

hoping to reach booking goals, which are used to set compensation levels, to "switch" these customers to higher-priced rooms.

7. Provide accurate information.
8. Be honest. Promote honesty, integrity, and high ethical standards.

Consumers choose hotel

As the lodging industry becomes more and more competitive, there is an increased need to understand the consumer. Many times advertising and promotional campaigns are created without taking into consideration how consumers actually make choices between competing properties. Many salespeople have a good understanding of what they are selling, but less understanding of how consumers evaluate what is being offered.

One variation on the theory of how consumers make decisions on what to buy is as follows:

1. Need arousal
2. Search for alternatives
3. Evaluation of alternatives/purchase
4. Usage and reevaluation

In each of the four stages, there are important elements that hotel managers and marketers should consider. It should be possible for these managers and marketers to control or manipulate certain aspects of these different stages to their benefit.

Need arousal

In order for the potential hotel guest to go through the purchase and usage process, there has to be a need or want that the purchase and usage will fulfil. Many of these needs are fairly easy to identify. A traveller needs a hotel room when visiting a city. A family wants to take a vacation. Most hotel managers/marketers are well aware of these different types of needs and wants.

Marketing implications. There are, however, two points that might not be so obvious. First, when travellers say they need a place to stay, what are they really saying? In point of fact, the traveller actually needs a place to sleep, or security, or comfort. The hotel manager and marketer must realize that there are many complex reasons underlying a traveller's need for a hotel room.

As a result hotel managers/marketers must try to identify the real reasons why people stay in hotels and cater to those wants and needs. Second, it is often useful when promoting a hotel to generate needs and wants the consumer might not independently think of. Why wait for consumers to arouse needs on they own? If consumers can be convinced they need a weekend getaway trip or vacation, a need created by the hotel managers/marketer, then the hotel benefits. As a result, one very important element in any advertising or promotional campaign is to *get people aroused to buy.* A lot of business can be lost if the hotel manager and marketer wait for the consumer to start the entire process.

Search for alternatives

After consumers are motivated by a need or want to buy, they usually will begin to search for alternative ways to satisfy those needs or wants. This search could be relatively quick and uncomplicated, relatively extensive and complex, or any level in between. Generally, the search and evaluation process would be short and uncomplicated if:

— The purchase is relatively inexpensive,

— The purchase is relatively unimportant,

— The purchase is relatively common, *and*

— The purchase is relatively easy to understand and use.

Alternatively, the search and evaluation process would be extensive and complex if:

— The purchase is relatively expensive,

— The purchase is relatively important,

— The purchase is relatively uncommon, or

— The purchase is relatively difficult to understand and use.

Compare the amount of effort a person might expend when searching for a budget motel for an overnight stay versus searching for an upscale resort hotel for a vacation. In the first case the purchase will be relatively inexpensive, probably not too personally important, fairly common in occurrence, and a pretty simple purchase. This person would not likely spend a lot of effort in searching for or evaluating alternative budget motels.

When this same person is looking for a vacation resort the situation changes. Now the purchase will be rather expensive. It will also have a lot of personal importance, because it is the person's vacation at stake. Similarly, the use of an upscale resort may be uncommon for the individual, and in general upscale resorts will have a lot more amenities and features to consider than budget motels.

Now this person will spend a lot more time reading brochures, talking to friends, speaking to travel professionals, and mulling over the options before making a final decision.

Marketing implications. From a marketing standpoint it should then be clear that, in the case of the budget motel, the consumer would be looking for basic information with which to make a quick decision. Generally, any quick reference would suffice. It may take nothing more than a readily available phone number to make the sale.

In the case of the resort much more information needs to be provided. The individual needs to look at a lot more information in order to be satisfied that all of the options have been considered.

Brochures have to be more attractive, salespeople have to be ready with lots of information, and in general the *risk* involved in marking such an important purchase has to be lessened. The process is more expensive and time consuming both from the standpoint of the consumer and the hotel.

Evaluation of alternatives/purchase

In most cases when people travel there are a number of competitive properties that are available to choose from. A great deal of research has been done on how people evaluate alternatives when choosing to buy a product or service. In marketing, the most widely researched evaluation model is the Fishbein and Ajzen model of reasoned action. In this theory we assume that every choice alternative has a series of attributes or characteristics that consumers will consider when choosing a particular alternative. For example, Hotel A might have the following attributes:

— Low price

— Good location

— No swimming pool

Similarly, Hotel B might have the following attributes:

— High price
— So-so location
— Swimming pool

Somehow, a consumer is going to have to make a decision as to which hotel to patronize.

In this most basic model, travellers evaluating different hotels would do so as a function of two factors. First, there is some assessment made as to the *desirability* of a certain attribute that the hotel may possess. Second, there is some *strength of belief* as to whether the hotel being evaluated actually possesses that attribute. An important part of the Fishbein model is that these two components would somehow be combined to provide the consumer with an overall evaluation—or attitude—for each hotel being assessed. An algebraic representation of this process is as follows:

$$A_o = \sum_{i=1}^{n} e_i b_i$$

where A_o = the overall attitude toward the alternative hotel

e_i = desirability of attribute i

b_i =the strength of belief that the alternative hotel possesses attribute i

n =the number of different attributes being evaluated

This algebraic model portrays the following process. Mentally, consumers assign values to the level of desirability and strength of belief elements of the model. For each attribute being considered, the desirability value and the belief strength value are multiplied, and then totalled for all the attributes considered. These mathematical totals are then compared, and the hotel with the most positive final total is the hotel the consumer would choose. As an example, consider the attributes listed above for Hotel A and Hotel B. Every consumer would have some opinion of the value of the price, location, and presence of a swimming pool. Similarly, every consumer would have some level of knowledge as to whether the individual property actually has these attributes. One way of quantifying how the consumer would decide which hotel to patronize is to assign numeric values to the desirability and belief strength values. Assume that for the desirability component the value can range from +5 for a highly desirable attribute to -5 for a highly undesirable attribute. Also assume that for the belief strength component the value could range from 0 for no belief the attribute exists to 10 for certainty the attribute exists. Now, assume that the following situation occurs. A traveller is looking for a hotel, and finds Hotel A and Hotel B. How is a choice between the two hotels made? For Hotel A the traveller believes that low price and good location are very positive considerations, but the absence of a swimming pool is also quite negative. For Hotel B the traveller thinks high prices and mediocre location are somewhat negative attributes, but a swimming pool is quite positive. Thus the *desirability levels* for both hotels' attributes, based on a scale of + 5 for very positive to - 5 for very negative, might appear as follows:

Hotel A	Hotel B
Price	+5 -3
Location	+5 -3
Swimming	-4 +4

Additionally, the traveller is somewhat sure that Hotel A has low prices, a good location, and a swimming pool. Alternatively, the traveller is not sure that Hotel B is expensive and has a so-so location, but is positive there is a swimming pool.

Thus the *belief strengths* concerning the presence of the attributes, based on a scale of + 10 for being positive the hotel has the attribute to 0 for being positive the hotel does not have the attribute, might appear as follows:

Hotel A	Hotel B	
Price	+6	+4
Location	+7	+5
Swimming Pool	+6	+10

Using the formula given above, the results would be as follows:

$$\text{Overall Evaluation}_{\text{Hotel A}} = (+5)(+6) + (+5)(+7) + (-4)(+6) = 41$$

$$\text{Overall Evaluation}_{\text{Hotel B}} = (-3)(+4) + (-3)(+5) + (+4)(+10) = 13$$

In this particular case, then, the traveller would pick Hotel A because the overall evaluation (41) is higher than the overall evaluation of Hotel B (13). Note that it is unlikely that people actually assign numerical values to the desirability levels or belief strengths. Rather, this kind of evaluation is probably done more casually, on the basis of feelings or impressions. Note also that this simple model has some elegance. If the consumer does not feel that a particular attribute is positive or negative, and therefore the desirability level is 0, the attribute would fall out of the equation. Similarly, if the consumer does not believe that the attribute exists, the belief strength would be 0, and the attribute would also fall out of the model.

Marketing implications. This model has several important implications for hotel managers/marketers. The goal is always to maximize your property's score relative to that of the competition, and this can be done in several ways. The manager and marketer of Hotel A can manipulate the components of the model, all with the goal of increasing the competitive strength of Hotel A. For example, the manager could try to:

— Increase the belief strengths for attributes of Hotel A consumers already think are desirable. (Advertise low rates and convenient location.)

— Increase the level of desirability for attributes. (Advertise the importance of location.)

— Introduce new attributes into the equation, minimizing the effect of existing negative attributes. (Advertise how good the room service is.)

— Decrease the belief strengths for attributes of Hotel B that consumers already think are desirable. (Advertise the fact that Hotel B's swimming pool is very small—more of a wading pool.)

— Decrease the level of desirability for attributes of Hotel B. (Advertise why a hotel swimming pool causes increased room rates.)

There are a number of different situations hotel managers/marketers would have to consider. First, not every consumer will have the same set of desirability levels or belief strengths. What marketing and sales professionals should be seeking are clusters of individuals that share essentially the same characteristics. Second, desirability levels can change easily. The fact that a swimming pool is an asset in the summer does not mean it is an asset in the winter. Care must be taken to fully assess the different variables that could have an impact on the desirability of a certain attribute.

Usage and reevaluation

Once a guest purchases the use of a hotel room the evaluation of the actual stay begins. Of course, there are a multitude of management issues involved in ensuring that the guest stay is positive. The marketing question here relates to how the guest actually evaluates the stay. One prevalent theory suggests that consumers create a series of expectations concerning the usage of what they buy. They then evaluate the actual performance of the purchase and compare that evaluation to their expectations. From this evaluation only two results can occur. If performance is greater than expectations then the guest will be satisfied. If expectations are greater than performance then the guest will be dissatisfied.

Marketing implications. If the guest is satisfied, then some positive behaviours might result.

First, the guest will start to become brand loyal. If the experience is good then presumably the guest will return repeatedly. This of course is the ultimate goal—to capture guests in such a way that they return and return.

Second, the guest usually will tell other people that the hotel is good. This is called *positive word-of-mouth advertising* and is one of the best types of advertising possible. Third, the guest might engage in other positive behaviours, such as writing letters of commendation to the management of the hotel. On the other hand, if the guest is dissatisfied, then some negative behaviours might occur. First, the guest probably will switch to another hotel. Second, the guest usually would tell other people that the hotel is not good. This is called *negative word-of-mouth advertising* and can be very damaging to the hotel. One interesting part of human nature is that people tend to listen to negative information more intently than positive information.

Third, the guest might engage in other negative behaviours like complaining to the front desk, writing complaint letters, contacting agencies like the Better Business Bureau, or, in an extreme case, suing the hotel.

There are a lot of complicated issues surrounding a discussion of how hotel guests go about choosing and evaluating a hotel. The system discussed in this chapter is not the only theoretical system in the marketing literature. However, many of the considerations outlined are very real problems that marketing managers need to assess.

The choice process is an enormously complicated one, and researchers certainly have not conclusively determined how each consumer acts in each situation.

An internal approach to hospitality marketing

The most important element of the hospitality product is not a tangible good (for example, a guest room or a meal) but the manner in which the "goods" of the hospitality industry are delivered. In survey after survey, hospitality consumers have underscored the importance of the service element—the manner in which the hospitality product is delivered—by placing good service foremost among the qualities they look for in a hotel or restaurant. Poor service is a recurring complaint among dissatisfied guests and the dominant theme of horror stories about unpleasant hotel stays.

Hospitality firms acknowledge the importance of high-quality service delivery, and many attempt to differentiate their product on service. It is a pervading theme in their advertising, marketing plans, training programs, and managerial edicts. Emphasizing service is one thing; delivering it is another. In fact, emphasizing service isn't the proper approach at all. The emphasis should be placed on the customer.

The internal customer

Since service delivery is an integral part of the hospitality product, employees' performance and attitudes play an essential role in selling the product. It is difficult for an employee to sell a product he or she does not believe in, so one of the first tasks of marketing and management should be to market the product—the hospitality operation and the role employees play in it—to the employee. From this insight emerges the concept of internal marketing, which views employees as a firm's internal customers and acknowledges the importance of satisfying these customers whose attitudes and performance are so crucial to the success of the operation.

Traditional marketing strategies—matching the product to the consumer, positioning the product correctly in the marketplace, establishing effective communication with the consumer, developing new products and features to satisfy the consumer and sustain his or her interest, studying the consumer's changing wants and needs, and, above all, creating a product that meets the needs and solves the problems of the consumer—should be applied first and foremost to the firm's internal customers, its employees.

Matching product to consumer

Some workers are intrinsically motivated and look for job satisfaction in the work itself. They work most productively when they are given the freedom to make decisions and exercise personal skills and talents that will add value to their work performance. Other employees are extrinsically motivated and obtain job satisfaction not from the work but from the salary, benefits, or other external rewards that accrue from performing the work.

Unlike the intrinsically motivated employee, extrinsically motivated workers work best when their tasks are clearly defined by their supervisors and do not require creativity or risk taking. Employees will be most satisfied with the product, their job, if management segments these internal customers by motivational style and markets the appropriate type of job to the appropriate employee.

The intrinsically motivated employee will seek innovative ways to satisfy the customer because customer satisfaction is an end in itself. On the other hand, extrinsically motivated persons will smile because they are told to do so—and doing what they are told is perceived as a means to an end. As a result, the extrinsically motivated employee may lose sight of what is important in providing a service, the root cause of the following incident.

A hotel sales manager books a bar mitzvah. The parents are concerned that everything go exactly right for this significant event. During the negotiations, the mother asks that the dinner plate that will be served be presented to her exactly as it will appear on the table. This done, the event is booked. On the day in question, the chef determines that this presentation will be detrimental to his food cost percentage. Without altering the quality of the product, he changes the plate to reduce the food cost. The mother is enraged.

The chef's motivation in this case was extrinsic. He considered the plate presentation a means to an end (low food costs) and not an end in itself (customer satisfaction). To stimulate intrinsic motivation, you should structure jobs in the following ways. Make them challenge the worker, test his or her valued abilities, and use a variety of skills. Allow the individual to participate in goal setting, scheduling, and developing procedures. Provide meaningful and informative feedback about how the job is going and make sure the worker can clearly identify the results of his or her work.

Communicating with the customer

To satisfy customers, we must understand what they need and expect. We, in turn, must effectively convey the nature of our product so customers will know what it is and how to use it. We need to maintain the same two-way communication with our internal customers. If our products, the jobs we offer, do not meet our internal customers' needs and expectations, they will go elsewhere or perform their jobs poorly. If we don't make the nature of our product clear, explaining the whys as well as the hows of jobs, our employees will not have the understanding of the product, their job, that will enable them to perform it well. Furthermore, employees will not "buy" the product when it appears that management is not willing to deliver on its promise of what it is "selling."

Creating new products

We compete with other operations for internal customers as well as external customers, and we must continually create new products to attract and keep them. We must offer better rates (that is, compensation), more attractive amenities (for example, benefits and awards), and a better product (for example, opportunities for advancement, schedules that meet our internal customers' needs, more challenging and interesting positions).

Our employees reflect the care with which we conduct our internal marketing. When we don't concern ourselves with satisfying our internal customers, they pass on their dissatisfaction to our external customers. A front desk clerk at a convention hotel gave this example: A large convention was checking into the hotel all day, and we never had a chance to get away from the desk for a coffee break or even for lunch. We were smiling for all we were worth, dealing with all the problems, and things were going pretty smoothly considering the circum-stances.

After a while, the nonstop demands started to get to us, though, and we devised a little sing-song communication and banter among ourselves that helped us to keep going and keep our sense of humour. While all this was going on, our supervisors were sitting in a room behind the front desk, talking and drinking coffee. Occasionally, one would step out and, seeing that everything was going well, go back to the coffee and conversation, leaving us to carry on.

When the supervisors heard our banter, though, everything changed. One of us was called into the back room and told to tell the others to cut it out. Our attitude changed immediately. We kept on working, but we no longer cared about the customers, and it showed. The front desk supervisors' lack of understanding and concern for their internal customers was immediately translated to lack of concern for the hotel's external customers, and, worst of all, anyone could tell.

The bonus

The advantages of internal marketing are twofold. If we satisfy our internal customers, they will be motivated to satisfy our paying customers, but the rewards of the internal-marketing approach do not end there. Internal marketing encourages a marketing orientation in a firm's employees. Even the employees who do not usually interact with the customer are a part of the marketing effort. It is the dishwasher who can stop a chipped glass from going back into the dining room. The storeroom employees can monitor the level of freshness of deliveries and ensure that perishable supplies are properly stored. The housekeeper can watch for burned-out light bulbs, and the engineer can ensure that heating and cooling systems and televisions are working properly.

All these employees contribute to the marketing effort, because they eliminate sources of dissatisfaction and help to keep customers. However, these employees often are unaware of their importance to the marketing effort and view their tasks simply as production activities. Through internal marketing, all employees can begin to understand how their tasks and the way they perform them affect customer satisfaction and contribute to a true marketing orientation.

Implementing internal marketing

To achieve maximum effectiveness as a marketing strategy, the internal-marketing concept must prevail throughout the organization. Human resources personnel introduce prospective employees to the firm's culture by marketing jobs from the customer perspective rather than the production perspective.

In an internal-marketing environment, the human resources department continues to stress the marketing perspective during employee training sessions by dividing training time between task-oriented technical instruction and service-oriented components that encourage employees to understand, relate to, and solve guests' problems. From the first contact, human resources staff members stress the employee's importance to the organization and the employee's personal impact on guests. This is not the widely practiced "smile training," but internal marketing. The success of the internal-marketing concept ultimately ties with management. Lower-level employees cannot be expected to be customer-conscious if the management above them does not display the same focus.

Operations-oriented managers who concern

themselves primarily with policies and procedures, often instituted without regard to the customer, undermine the firm's internal-marketing effort, reducing employees' jobs to mechanical functions that offer little in the way of challenge, self-esteem, or personal gratification. Moreover, by requiring employees to adhere rigidly to specific procedures, the operations-oriented manager ties their hands and restricts their ability to satisfy customers, as the following situations demonstrate.

> As a promotional tactic, a hotel in a national, upscale chain presented guests at checkin with a free-drink voucher to be redeemed at the revolving rooftop lounge. The complimentary-drink offer seemed an ideal way to market the hotel while merchandising the lounge. A couple who had been given the free-drink voucher returned to the hotel around midnight and decided to go to the lounge for a nightcap. The lounge was nearly empty. Inspired by a table tent promoting ice-cream drinks, one of the couple decided to have some ice cream instead of a drink. When she took the order, the waitress informed the couple that she couldn't serve plain ice cream, because ice cream was only served in drinks.

Interpreting the waitress's resistance as a desire to "build the check," the couple said they would pay for the drink if the waitress would bring only the ice cream. The waitress, very friendly and wearing her most hospitable smile, told them she couldn't do that because it was against the hotel's policy.

The service in the lounge (and similar incidents) cost the hotel those two customers and possibly other potential customers who heard the disgruntled couple's story. The couple may have had positive feelings toward the hotel at the time they received their free-drink voucher, but the effectiveness of the voucher as a marketing device was lost because the service the couple received when they went to the lounge to redeem it was frustrating and irritating.

Making an exception to the chlorinating policy to meet the needs of the hot, tired guests would have been good marketing, but the pool attendant's supervisor was operations-oriented rather than marketing-oriented and was more concerned with following procedure than satisfying guests. That focus cost the hotel 32 customers immediately and lost that conference group's repeat business as well. There must be policies to guide employees' actions, but management cannot sell employees a marketing approach if it practices an operational approach and denies them the freedom and flexibility to use their judgment to solve customers' problems and meet their needs.

Employees who are encouraged to respond to customers' needs but are denied the right to do so will recognize lip service when they hear it and cease to believe in the so-called customer-oriented product they are being asked to sell. Some managers may argue that policies and procedures are developed to ensure that the operation functions smoothly and guests receive consistent service, but where people are concerned, it is impossible to anticipate every situation in advance and develop appropriate policies for every employee-guest interaction.

Although it is management's role to develop policies and procedures that will keep the hotel running smoothly, it must recognize that individualized, personal interactions are the essence of high-quality service and allow employees some freedom to respond to situations that arise. When the internal-marketing orientation of their organization helps employees on every level to appreciate that the needs of people are foremost, then they are prepared to participate in another marketing strategy that is played out inside the house—relationship marketing.

The external customer

Relationship marketing focuses on the external customer and is directed toward protecting a firm's customer base. In this approach, the customer is recognized as an asset, and the focus is directed toward maintaining and enhancing customer relationships. When the business of a firm is selling service, the buyer-seller relationship becomes paramount. When the service being sold is hospitality, the quality of the buyer-seller relationship is of such importance that it may supersede the other components of the product and alone determine the perceived quality of the product. Yet, it is common for hospitality firms to concentrate their marketing efforts on obtaining new customers and to do a poor job of handling their relationships with current customers. At some properties, in fact, customers are treated with so little consideration and are given such poor and reluctant service that it would seem the staff regards them as liabilities to be disposed of as quickly as possible.

For instance, a major complaint among meeting planners is that there is no one at the hotel to handle their problems once their meeting is under way, although there was ample staff to wine and dine them with the greatest attention before the meeting was booked. A marketing focus that is directed only toward media advertising and other external promotion is shortsighted and self-defeating, since the customer's experience at a property is the firm's most potent advertising. Consider the case of a hotel of a major international chain that spends tens of thousands of dollars on advertising and promotion:

A couple went to a hotel located near their home for a long weekend following their December marriage. December was a slow period for the hotel, and occupancy at that time was traditionally as low as 20 percent. The couple returned to the hotel to celebrate their anniversary on the three subsequent years, each time spending about $500. They also stayed at the hotel or ate dinner there as often as three or four times during the year, occasionally accompanied by other couples. The couple returned for their fourth anniversary and were welcomed by the desk clerk, who knew them from previous stays. After they were settled in their room, they called the dining room to see how late they could get room service. They were informed that the dining room and, kitchen were closed for the employees' annual Christmas party. When they asked why they weren't told that there would be no food service when they made their reservation so they could have stopped on the way to the hotel for dinner, or why the desk clerk had not informed them before they went to their room, changed out of their street clothes, and opened their champagne, they were given no satisfactory answer. Their anniversary dinner consisted of two chicken sandwiches they managed to coax out of someone in the kitchen.

The following morning, a false fire alarm forced them out of their room and down to the lobby in their nightclothes. For this inconvenience, they were given a complimentary cup of coffee. When they checked out three days later, the husband asked for the room discount to which he was entitled through membership in an organization that had an agreement with the hotel. The clerk informed him that he could not have the discount because he had not requested it when checking in. That stipulation was part of the agreement, but the husband had forgotten to mention the discount on checkin. The couple were confident that there would be no problem obtaining the discount, because the hotel personnel knew them from their previous visits, and they had always used the discount.

Although the clerk knew them and had checked them in personally, he would not grant them the discount. He said that only the general manager had the authority to authorize the discount retroactively, and the general manager was not on the premises. The discount was not large, but the customer was still so upset when he returned home that he wrote to the general manager, asking for the discount and describing the inconveniences that had marked the couple's stay. In a two-page letter the GM informed him that fire alarms were for the safety of guests, explained why employees should have Christmas parties, and flatly denied the customer's request for his discount.

The customer then wrote to the vice president of marketing of the hotel's franchiser, enclosing a copy of the GM's letter. Shortly afterward, he received a second letter from the GM, opening with the statement, "We are always glad to know of our customers' complaints because it helps us to improve our operations," and ending with an invitation to spend a weekend at the hotel as a guest of the general manager.

The relationship between the hotel and this customer was past repairing, however, and the customer never went back. Some of his friends no longer patronize the hotel on the basis of this story, and it is impossible to estimate just how far this damaging word of mouth spread or how much business the hotel lost through this one couple's unpleasant experience. To avoid granting a discount that amounted to approximately $25, this hotel sacrificed its relationship with a valuable customer who had patronized the hotel regularly during a time of low occupancy and brought in business year round. This decision was the antithesis of relationship marketing, which focuses on the customers we have rather than just the customers we hope to acquire.

Relationship marketing means keeping a customer because of his or her relationship to your operation. It is not a matter of giving something away that you would not otherwise. In fact, if a relationship with a hotel is strong, a customer might be willing to pay more because of it. Relationship marketing is a natural extension of internal marketing. When the work environment reflects the message that people are important, employees will be guest-oriented rather than task-oriented.

When management exerts a concerted effort to satisfy employees by stressing their importance to the success of the organization, responding to their needs, and rewarding their efforts, employees will be motivated to satisfy guests. When employees understand how their job contributes to the guest's experience, and they are given the latitude to do their job precisely in the way that will most please the guest, their job performance becomes a matter of personal pride, and the guest's satisfaction becomes a personal reward.

No advertising or promotional campaign, no matter how appropriate or clever, can market your operation as effectively as an enthusiastic guest. On the other hand, no campaign, no matter how poorly conceived, can discourage potential customers as surely as a disgruntled guest.

When formulating your long-range marketing plan, you would do well to incorporate the nontraditional approach—starting your marketing efforts from the inside, where the loyalty of guests is won or lost. Internal marketing creates a hospitality environment in which guests find solutions, not problems, and furthers the development of a service-oriented staff that is aware of its impact on customers and is motivated to give personal attention to customers' comfort and satisfaction.

Hotel pricing

The classical analysis explaining price in terms of supply and demand has passed through many examinations and revisions, but still stands in its essential idea as the most satisfactory, most generally acceptable explanation of the phenomena of price determination.

Key elements for pricing decisions

All pricing decisions are based on the economic principles of supply and demand. More specifically, demand relative to available supply on any given day determines the price in the marketplace. This basic tenet of economic theory holds as true for the sale of a hotel guest room as it does for the sale of a loaf of bread, a life insurance policy, and a college education. The essential elements of price theory include demand, competition, and cost.

Demand

Demand determines the highest rate that can be charged, that is, "what the market will bear." Some business travellers to New York City are willing to pay a $300+ daily room rate for first-class accommodations in midtown Manhattan. Some families will pay up to $5,000 a week for a family vacation at a fantasy resort in the Hawaiian Islands. College students going downhill skiing for a weekend may put their "ceiling" at $10 per night.

Demand from any identified target market will fluctuate. Business travel tends to be heaviest in the fall and spring, and, not surprisingly, hotel rates for this market peak during these time periods. Vacation travel of Canadians to Florida is particularly strong in the winter months. So are the rates they pay.

Education associations like to meet during the summer months, when school is out of session. This market is also fairly price sensitive. Thus, hotels targeting to business travellers in the fall, winter, and spring may target the education segment as a secondary market in the summer at lower rates.

Demand determines the high end of a rate structure, depending on who the target market is and its price sensitivities. Yet this is just a start. Competition in the marketplace, and the costs incurred by these suppliers, also have a major impact on final pricing decisions.

Competition

Competition can be viewed from both a direct and indirect perspective. Indirect competition refers to the broad range of alternatives available to travellers. Vacationers have the option of staying with friends and relatives, camping, or simply making day trips close to home.

In other words, they have an option not to purchase a hotel room for overnight accommodations. The same holds true for business travellers. They, too, have the option of day trips only, or shortened trips of a one- to two-day duration. Indeed, the average night's stay for an individual business traveller is typically 1.3 nights. Overnight couriers, fax machines, and the like have made the decision to even take a business trip in the first place a questioned business expense. A hotel's direct competition comes from those hotels that compete for similar target markets. Sheraton, Marriott, and Hyatt, for example, a compete on a national level for the upscale business traveller, including independent, corporate, and convention business travel.

In many respects, this market views these suppliers of hotel accommodations as close substitutes—or viable alternatives—when making a decision on where to book their room. Though the price of that room is only one of several factors in making the decision on where to stay, it is a salient and important factor. Suppliers who deviate from an acceptable relevant range will eventually lose potential customers to their competition. Competition is a key element in putting a cap, or parameters, on the relevant range of prices. When demand exceeds supply in the marketplace—known as peak demand periods—the relevant range is higher on the demand/competition/cost continuum. And conversely, when supply exceeds demand—known as off-peak periods or valley demand periods—the relevant range of prices is usually much lower. For example, in the Boston market first-class hotel convention rates can range from $150 to $200 during the September, October, May, and June peak periods. Yet, in the slower winter months, room rates offered to the convention market can fall much lower, to the $100 to $125 range. Experienced convention buyers are well aware of these price variations in the hotel business, or rather, its peak and valley fluctuations. Hotel price decision makers need to monitor the market closely, anticipate as best they can high and "soft" periods; and avoid the pitfalls of the "we don't discount" syndrome. This syndrome, especially when hotels practice it in valley periods, can result in lost business, missed budgets, and unhappy owners.

Discounting during off-peak periods in the hotel business is common. Different target markets have varying elasticities of demand, and, thus, when supply exceeds demand, astute hotel management looks to the more elastic demand segments to fill their hotel rooms.

Discounting utilizes the fact that varying elasticities of demand do exist, and that the more elastic markets, such as educators, are willing to buy at discounted rates.

Elastic markets, by definition, are the more price-sensitive demand segments that purchase greater quantities at lower prices. Discounted hotel room rates are a direct application of the economic principles of elasticity of demand.

Cost

There are essentially two kinds of costs for any business enterprise—fixed costs and variable costs. Fixed costs are the costs of "being" in business, and they remain the same regardless of business volume. The variable costs are the costs of "doing" business, and they vary with business volume (materials, direct labour, and so forth). Though there are a number of semivariable and semifixed costs associated with running a business, the purpose here is to distinguish between the short-run costs of doing business and the long-run costs of being in business. The short-run, or variable, costs for hotel guest rooms are largely housekeeping labour, bathroom amenities, laundry, and the like. It is essentially the cost of an occupied room.

Variable costs in the hotel industry are relatively low, ranging from $20 to $75 per room per night depending on the service level of the hotel (budget, midtier, luxury), the location (metropolitan, suburban, resort), and the occupancy of the hotel (during high-occupancy periods hotels often incur overtime labour costs). To give an example, variable costs for full-service hotels in metropolitan areas can range from $30 to $60 per occupied room per night.

It is the variable costs that are relevant to the pricing decision. These daily costs of doing business need to be covered and thus are the minimum threshold for room-rate pricing decisions. Any revenue exceeding these costs contributes something to the fixed overhead, which is better than no contribution at all. It makes no sense (both intuitively and financially) to sell a room for $25 if the variable cost to sell that room is $30. Most hoteliers recognize that profit margins can and will be lower in the off-peak periods.

Contribution margins are simply lower during the slower periods, yet nonetheless contribute something to the fixed overhead costs of being in business. During peak demand periods, contribution margins are greater and thus contribute significantly to the fixed costs of the hotel operation. It is in the long run, cutting across both peak and off-peak demand periods, that successful management realizes reasonable profits.

Profits vary across business cycles as well. Contribution margins can be very low during a recession period, as the hotel industry experienced during the early 1990s. Even with deeply discounted room rates, special promotions, and aggressive selling, hotels worldwide faced a sharp decline in demand.

Business travel was down, pleasure travel was almost nonexistent. Staying in business was a matter of survival and not necessarily profitable. Economic stability has to occur before profitability can be realized. In the meantime, sell what you can at a price the customer is willing to pay, as long as the price meets or exceeds the basic costs of "doing" business.

Pricing as a marketing decision

Pricing is a marketing decision. And marketing's mandate is customer satisfaction. Indeed, charging the right price is clearly part of that mandate. Marketing is giving the target customers what they want, when they want it, where they want it, at a price they are willing and able to pay. The pricing decision needs to be made within the context of the consumer, and not in the confines of the accounting department. It is through customer satisfaction that long-run profit goals are realized. Pricing is viewed in different ways by different constituencies. For example, liquidity issues are of concern to hotel owners.

To hotel managers, realities of the marketplace are of primary concern. Yet to the consumer, pricing means what they are willing and able to pay to rent a room for the night. The customer doesn't care about liquidity issues, financial statements, or return on investment. Nor does the customer care about market share battles among suppliers in the marketplace. What the customer does care about is a hotel room for the night that is clean and secure—at a good price for value as perceived by that buyer.

Market positioning

Customer perception is what positioning is all about. There is much truth to the adage "perception is reality." If the customer thinks the price is too high, it is, regardless of what the owners and managers think. The same holds true if a price is perceived to be too low. Price is a signal of quality. Too low a price can signal poor quality whether the quality is good or not. Positioning enters the demand/competition/ cost continuum as both a minimum and maximum threshold for the hotel room-rate pricing decision. If your rates are perceived to be too high (within a product class such as the midtier hotel market) the customers will go elsewhere. If your rates are perceived to be too low, no one will come. In either case, profits will, of course, not be realized.

Positioning decisions, made by senior-level management, set the parameters for the relevant range of prices for a hotel. Actual price decisions, depending on the target market, will lie somewhere within that predetermined range. The term "rack rate" refers to the upper end of the range, often called "list price" in other industries.

Deep discounts or special package rates are at the lower end of the range. If the rack rates are too high and/or discounts too low, the overall image or "positioning" of the hotel is in jeopardy. A good example to demonstrate this point is the emergence of the weekend package. Now commonly referred to as the weekend package market, it consists, essentially, of highly discounted rates directed to pleasure travellers and local residents to help boost weekend occupancies. Metropolitan hotels primarily cater to business travellers, who are abundant during the week but absent on the weekends. Hotels needed a way to attract people during these "softer" periods at a price that would not fall below the variable costs. The strategy is to reach out to a more price-sensitive market with a lower price, but not so low as to compromise your position in the marketplace. Hotels are not willing to risk their image as perceived by their primary target market, which in this case is the weekday business traveller. Thus, the concept of the weekend package market was born. Local residents and pleasure travellers who cannot afford to stay at a hotel for $150 per night can afford $90 per night when it is perceived as a good price for value. Just as importantly, the business traveller does not feel ripped off when he or she hears of these special weekend package rates.

In fact, a large portion of the weekend package market is the business-person who is travelling for pleasure on the weekends. Hotel management realizes that individuals will surface in multiple target markets, depending on the purpose of the trip. They also realize that the price sensitivities (or price elasticities) of these individuals will vary, depending on the purpose of the trip as well.

Yield management

Yield management, or revenue management, grew in popularity throughout the 1980s and will continue to do so well into the 1990s and beyond. Though the term is relatively new, the concept itself has been practiced for quite some time. Advanced computer technology has spurred the increased acceptance and use of yield management in hospitality management today. Yield management, in hotel vernacular, is a systematic (automated) approach to pricing decisions through guest room inventory management and the prices allocated to each room in that inventory. Its primary objective is revenue maximization for any given day (or period). In other words, depending on forecasted demand for a future period, prices are adjusted to reflect that demand. Yield management essentially adjusts the price of the available guest room inventory to reflect the realities of the marketplace.

Forecasting is key to the successful implementation of a yield-management system. Most hotels target multiple markets, each of which has a different price elasticity of demand. Through automation, and using the computer, hotel managers can capture the subtleties of market shifts (shifts in forecasted demand) and adjust the prices of the remaining rooms inventory to ensure that rooms do not go unsold,

Conversely, when demand is higher than expected for the higher-rated room categories, the number of available rooms in the discounted room category is reduced. For example, an initial forecast may show 100 rooms to be sold at a rack rate of $150, and 100 rooms to be sold at a discounted convention rate of $120. However, a revised forecast may show demand for the rack-rated rooms to be lower than expected. A yield-management system would automatically signal this revised forecast and reallocate 20 of the 100 rack-rated rooms to the discounted convention room inventory.

In other words, the rack-rated room inventory would now be 80 rooms and the discounted convention room inventory would be 120 rooms. This is done to ensure maximum *revenues,* or the highest "yield," for the given period. The primary assumption here is that the 20 rack-rated rooms would have gone unsold unless their price was reduced, or opened up to the discounted convention rate market. Again, the objective of yield management is revenue maximization. Getting the best price, relative to supply and demand conditions for a given period, is the goal.

Pricing as a customer decision

Demand, competition, and cost all play an important role in the hotel room-rate pricing decision. Demand sets the ceiling and costs set the floor. Competition, or supply relative to demand, helps determine more precisely how high or how low a price will be. Positioning, or how you want to be perceived in the marketplace, sets the upper and lower limits of the price range to be offered. Some hotels may have wider ranges than others, depending on the desired position to be achieved.

Pricing decisions are made every day in the reservation and front office departments. What it does mean is that the customer is the one who really makes the decision. And it is our job as marketing-minded hoteliers to find out just what it is that the customer really wants and at what price he or she is willing and able to pay. It is a tenet of marketing that the customer is always right.

Market positioning

Market positioning is the natural followthrough of

market segmentation and target marketing. In fact, a hotel's position should be built on its target markets, because the advertisements proclaiming a position should be aimed at the chosen targets. Today, many lodging and restaurant firms are quite conscious of their position, and they are using their advertising to declare that position. What's clear from most hotel advertising is that many lodging companies have not figured out how to state their position in a customer-oriented way.

Objective positioning

Objective positioning is concerned almost entirely with the physical attributes of your product. This advertising copy platform creates an image of your property that reflects its physical characteristics and functional features. The following are examples of an objective position: Motel 6 offers low-cost rooms; the Cerromar Beach Hotel is on the ocean; Ponderosa Steak House sells steaks; the Chicago Hilton is a large downtown hotel. These positions conjure up clear, objective images, two of them indicated by the names.

Objective positioning need not be concrete, however. The Ritz Carlton is a luxury hotel; the Chicago Hilton is a convention hotel; McDonald's is clean; Lutece provides a gourmet experience. Again, these images are clear and objective, but they derive from the product itself. Objective product positioning is important and is used often in the hospitality industry—successfully in the following examples.

The key to objective positioning is that your characteristic must be unique in some way. Too often, however, the characteristic that hotels promote is not unique. This is why many hotel ads that show building exteriors fail to create an image or differentiate the property.

Subjective positioning

When you try to influence people's perceptions of your operation, you are dealing with subjective positioning. The perceived image of your property does not belong to the product; it is connected with the consumer's mental processes. Moreover, the subjective image may not necessarily reflect the true state of the product's physical characteristics. With image advertising, you are trying to align perceptions with the image you want to project. Hilton's slogan, America's Business Address, is an example of an attempt at subjective positioning. Since there are many other business hotels, Hilton's proposition is not unique and may fail to differentiate it from other operations. Looking again at the Garden City Hotel ad, it is effective because it takes objective criteria and makes them subjective.

Tangible positioning

The difficulty with creating images for hotels is considering an image a tangible product. Most hotels in a given product class are eminently interchangeable in the customer's mind. We refer to that condition as being a commodity or a near commodity. The challenge of hotel advertising, then, is to create a unique, intangible mental picture of a product that is mostly tangible and not particularly unique.

Intangible positioning

The complexity of the hospitality business is that a part of it is, indeed, intangible. In fact, the part we really want to market is not tangible—it is the experience of staying at the hotel or the enjoyment of eating a steak. No one can take a hotel stay home to use. So, while we must create perceptions for our bricks and mortar, we must also give solid evidence of the intangible experience we sell. Such intangible elements are all very abstract. Alas, the evidence we can adduce to sell the customers our intangible experience is quite similar from company to company.

Promoting benefits

With your position, you promise certain benefits to the customer and offer solutions to the customer's problems. The benefits and solutions should, if at all possible, be different and better than the competition's. The Embassy Suites campaign featuring Garfield differentiates the chain by promoting benefits that guests will appreciate.

Positioning goes deeper than advertising. It should be a singleminded concept, an umbrella under which everything else in the organization sits. As hotel marketer William Dowling explains: "Properly targeted, singleminded positioning affects everything a hotel [or restaurant] does or stands for—not only advertising, but also all of its promotions, brochures, facilities, and even its decor." Dowling should have included policies and procedures, employees' attitudes, customer relations, complaint handling, and all the other aspects of your operation that combine to make the hospitality experience.

Positioning plays a vital role in the development of the entire marketing mix. It also provides the necessary consistency among the elements of your operation.

Controlling the spin

Your customers will form an opinion of your position whether you have one or not. Uncontrolled, this subjective position may mean that your firm is lumped together with totally dissimilar operations. Your challenge is to control the consumer's perception of your position. Moreover, if you fail to select a position, you may face one of several undesirable consequences, as enumerated by Christopher Lovelock:

1. Your firm or some of its products will be pushed into a position where they face head-on competition from stronger competitors.
2. Your firm ends up in a position that no one wants because there is little customer demand for such a firm or product.
3. Your firm's position is so fuzzy that no one knows what you do well.
4. Your firm will have no position at all in the marketplace because no one has heard of it.

Consequently, you must choose an effective position that clearly distinguishes you from competitors on factors that are important to your target market.

Repositioning

A firm may have many reasons for repositioning. It may occupy an unsuccessful position, or it may face competition that is too strong or too numerous in its current position. The firm may also see an opportunity for taking advantage of a new market niche. John A. Hurley has explained how repositioning can be part of a turnaround plan. In any event, repositioning operates just like the original positioning process, except that the old position must be removed from consumers' perceptions. Many firms have tried to reposition, with various levels of success.

To avoid direct competition with McDonald's, some hamburger chains have repositioned as "gourmet hamburger" restaurants. Friendly's, originally positioned for ice cream and sandwiches, failed in its attempt to reposition as a family restaurant. Howard Johnson's tried to move into two positions at once. It tried to keep its identity as a family restaurant and also change to a young adult restaurant with a bar and live music. The move served only to tarnish further an already weak image.

Boston park plaza

Repositioning is often needed to save a hotel property, as in the case of the Boston Park Plaza, nee the Statler Hotel. This was the central hotel of the city, the one where all the grand events occurred. This property was the Statler Hotel until Hilton took it over and it became the Hilton Hotel. Many years had taken their toll. Rooms were small and dingy. Bathrooms were antiquated. Public facilities were tired and limited. The entire property was tired and old. Hilton ran it for a few years, lost money on it, and decided to give up the ghost. The hotel was awaiting the wrecker's ball when it obtained a last-minute reprieve from the Saunders brothers of Boston, who felt the hotel was too much of a landmark to be destroyed. They bought the hotel, under the aegis of Hotels of Tradition, and completely renovated it.

The marketing problem was one of positioning, letting the public know that this was a "new" hotel, completely renovated and ready to compete in today's market.

The task of reaching Boston travellers, who had long since forsaken the hotel for more modern properties, would be monumental and expensive. The owners took a different approach. They marketed it to the locals as a modern hotel of tradition. The locals told the visitors. This was a successful repositioning effort.

The Waldorf

The effort of the Waldorf-Astoria is another example of repositioning. The Waldorf was perceived as a hotel of royalty and top business executives. Although it was in the same price range as its competition, it was perceived as expensive. As shown in the accompanying ad, the

Waldorf wanted to reposition to reach middle managers also. The repositioning campaign emphasized their lifestyles, along with the affordability and attributes of the Waldorf.

A repositioning effort, then, should use the following procedure.

— *First, you must determine your present position.* It is essential to know where you are now before you determine how you are going to get to where you want to go. In repositioning, it is critical to find out what the consumer thinks of your operation, because the consumer's image might not be what you think it is. Before trying to change a perception, you have to know what that perception is.

— *Determine what position you wish to occupy.* This step calls for thorough research of the market, the competition, and the resources your company has to occupy the position. Thorough and objective research will help you avoid the trap of wishful thinking. You must make certain your new position is truly different.

— *Initiate the repositioning campaign,* based on the three criteria of effective positioning: image, differentiation, and promised benefits.

— *Assess whether your position has changed in the consumer's eyes.* It is naive to assume that perceptions have changed simply because you expect them to change. Changes in sales or profit figures are not a measure of whether your repositioning was successful, because these figures may be influenced by other factors.

Price

Price can be a powerful positioning tool. By itself, however, price does not truly differentiate market segments, especially within the same general product class. On the other hand, price can play a large role in differentiating between different product classes. The power of price positioning is one reason that upscale hotel chains maintain high rack rates and then discount them severely.

Lowering the official price might also lower the image. The danger in this approach is that the unsuspecting potential customer might not realize that the discount is available, thereby forming the perception that this company's hotels are out of reach.

Positioning multiple brands

To maintain their growth rates, many companies have developed multiple brands that are supposed to have unique positions that appeal to different market segments. The problem is to position each brand so that one does not cannibalize another.

Market positioning is a valuable weapon for hospitality marketers. Creating a successful position requires recognition of the marketplace, the competition, and consumers' perceptions. If you research the wants and needs of your target market, you will have the tools to identify opportunities for creating the desired image that differentiates you from the competition and for serving your target market better than anyone else.

4

Menu Development

The most important management area of any restaurant operation is the menu program. It is the major key to the profitability and success of an operation. The menu program involves every aspect of an operation from purchasing to accounting and directly affects the quality of both food products and guest service. It consists of all of the elements of the planning, production, and sales analysis of menu items, including the printed menu.

Once the style of restaurant operation and average check have been determined, management can begin to plan the basic content of the menu so that the selection of kitchen equipment, facilities design and layout, pricing and cost controls, purchasing and distribution plans, labour requirements, training programs, and computer food service systems can take place.

An essential ingredient in the menu program is cuisine. Cuisine is the style or manner in which food is prepared and is usually associated with a specific nationality or region of a country. The style of restaurant operation determines a level of service and food preparation. Cuisine selection directly affects cooking methods and purchasing requirements for the food products needed. Equipment availability determines the type of method that can be used for food preparation. The cooking load, or amount of food product that can be prepared at any one time, is determined by the variety of cooking equipment available in a kitchen.

Labour resources in a community are a major factor in the selection of both a style of restaurant operation and the sophistication of the preparation methods planned for menu items. As one of the major areas of concern facing restaurateurs in the 1990s, labour and food service skill level availability is of primary importance to a menu program. The menu repertory is an index of all of the food items that could be prepared in a restaurant and serves as a major quality control factor in daily operations. The selection of food items is controlled by the availability of food product and the capacity of the restaurant to store it properly to ensure the least amount of waste through spoilage and theft.

Establishing standards becomes a management priority for an ongoing restaurant operation. Two basic standards relate to food quality and service.

Standards of food quality include a variety of concerns regarding food purchasing, storage, distribution, preparation, presentation, and costing. Standards of service include wait service, customer service, and restaurant presentation, important aspects of a successful operation.

Cuisine

The diversity of cuisines offered in the American restaurant of the 1990s is a direct result of the food service customer of the 1980s. Their demand for more diversity in cuisine offerings at all levels of restaurant styles from quick service to fine dining resulted in the current range of menu offerings. Combinations of food products and cooking methods in the 1980s were highly experimental as chefs competed for customer attention.

American nouvelle cuisine

What began as a return to regional native American foods and food combinations has become an eclectic combination of fresh food products, cultures, and cuisines. The layering of one cuisine on another is producing menu combinations which are at times as startling for their diversity as the variety of tastes and presentations that they produce.

It is not uncommon to find a full service restaurant offering menu selections in all categories from appetizer to dessert that represent a gathering of a half dozen American and international cuisines.

Southwestern/Mexican cuisine

The southwestern/ Mexican cuisine trend began across most of the United States with basic food items such as tacos, burritos, and enchiladas. The restaurant chain Chili's has expanded these menu offerings to include a variety of frahitas and sizzling steak platters in a casual dining setting. Grilling over mesquite coals also became popular in the 1980s, and although the use of mesquite as a cooking fuel has tapered off, grilling as a cooking method has become increasingly popular.

Heartful dining

Called by many names, "healthly eating" has become a firmly established menu concept of the 1990s and one that should influence every menu. Originally this trend responded to customer needs for foods prepared with cooking methods that did not involve frying or use of heavy sauces and were low in sodium and free of preservatives. Today it has become a major concern of the American dining public.

Quick meals

A definite change in eating patterns, called "quick meals," has evolved. This trend is appearing both in the daily meal pattern for individuals and in the way in which menu items are selected from a menu to make up a meal. The traditional pattern of three major meals a day is changing to five or six small meals, or quick bites, consumed in the following general time pattern throughout the day:

7:00 a.m.: Light breakfast

10:30 a.m.: Midmorning snack

2:00 p.m.: Light lunch

5:30 p.m.: Small meal

9:00 p.m.: Late evening snack

The major characteristic of food items for small meals is a reduction in the portion size of the main item and a change in the selection of the surrounding items such as heavy starches and sauces. Food manufacturers are responding to consumer needs on the supermarket level by providing a wide variety of proportioned and pre-prepared small meals that can be microwaved.

On the restaurant level, "quick bites" involve choosing two or three appetizers, soups, and/or salads to make up the major portion of the meal rather than the traditional appetizer with main course and surrounding items. Menu items are often shared by diners, making the meal an entertainment function.

Paolo's menu concentrates on Italian cuisine items cooked in a wood burning oven or on an open grill. Restaurant managers have found that this trend in menu selection often produces the same check or a higher average check than the traditional format.

Equipment capacity

Ongoing restaurants have equipment which must either be incorporated into food preparation methods or replaced with more functional pieces. Before making any menu selections a complete evaluation of current equipment and its capabilities should be made.

Management must now look at the food preparation methods most commonly applied to the production of menu items in the style and level of cuisine that they have selected. An evaluation of what equipment will be needed in addition to that already in place will help management to determine the feasibility of any changes in the current menu offerings.

Table 1
Quick Meal Menu Selection

Diner One	Diner Two
Minestrone soup	Mussels marinara
Fried calamari	Carpaccio Milanese
Roman chicken	Ravioli
Caesar salad	Paolo's salad
Chocolate mousse torte	Kiwi lime sorbet
Espresso	Cappuccino
Total check, $26.05	Total check, $29.30

Labour needs are as important to equipment selection as food preparation. The skill levels of available food production employees in your community often determine the type of preparation equipment that is needed. The amount of preprepared product that is incorporated into purchasing specifications will also help to reduce equipment needs. For example, a buffalo chopper, or spinning bowl food cutter, can in one minute process six heads of cabbage or six pounds of celery or five pounds of onions. The equipment requires kitchen space of 33 by 24 inches. Processed produce will need to be washed, trimmed, and cut to size for chopping and slicing. Kitchen staff will need to be able to prepare produce with a processing.

The alternative is a wide variety of high-quality precut and sliced vegetables, which are packaged without additives, have a good shelf life, and are ready for immediate use in a wide variety of recipes.

.Equipment can also offer management the ability to develop menu items using product that is high in both food cost and prepreparation labour costs. An excellent example of this is shrimp.

Regardless of the size, shrimp needs to be preprepared by deveining and often shelling. Individual handling of shrimp breaks down the product and is labour-intensive.

The alternative is to use a shrimp peeling and deveining machine, which is cost-effective when 500 pounds of shrimp a week are put into production. Using the peeling and deveining machine allows management to purchase at bulk prices when buying large quantities of shrimp and take advantage of fluctuating prices on various sizes of shrimp.

Labour capacity

The capacity of labour to produce the menu items selected for a restaurant menu is a major management concern.

Without the professional culinary skills to prepare and produce menu items management is forced to select items which can be prepared with a maximum amount of preprepared food products. The cooking methods required for these menu items must also utilize equipment such as microwave and convection ovens and fryalators.

In many cases a skilled chef is available, but the remainder of the kitchen crew has little or no training. In this situation management must select menu items and ingredients that allow the chef to concentrate on those aspects of preparation and presentation that create an important menu item. Effective planning for this labour situation can result in a menu which blends uncomplicated listings with recipes that can become signature items, highlighting the experienced chef to the benefit of the restaurant.

Table 2
Shrimp production rate by pounds per hour

Shrimp Count (Number per Pound)	Pounds per Hour
16/202	10-275
36/42	100-120
51/60	70-85
Shrimp Production Rate by Hand for Skilled Worker	
43/50	1 lb per hour
Time per shrimp	11/4 shrimp per minute
Labour cost based on $5.50 per hour	11 cents per shrimp

The menu repertory

The menu repertory is an index of all of the food items that could be prepared in a restaurant and serves as a major quantity control factor in daily operations. In each category any item that the restaurant can prepare is listed. Additional recipe and cost card files are created to merge with this listing so that management can select menu items at any time that have been evaluated as to their potential success in both customer satisfaction and profitability. These items are chosen on the basis of a selection process outlined in the following list:

Menu repertory selection outline

A. General item selection

B. Problem identification

C. Repertory item selection

D. Final menu selection

Step A is the listing of any food item that could be prepared in the restaurant under the guidelines of restaurant style, cuisine, equipment, and labour availability.

Step B in the repertory selection process identifies any items for which there may be a problem finding product, preparing, or serving. This category also requires that management evaluate the costs of the food products and the resulting menu price. If the price will be too high to balance with the other menu items, then it must be eliminated.

Step C chooses a number of menu items for each category which offers an interesting but compatible selection from which management can choose a final menu. Those items not listed on the printed menu now become available as menu specials and backup items to utilize seasonal ingredients and reconstitute leftover food. These items can also be test marketed through the menu "specials" program that registers customer reaction to menu items.

Step D, the final menu selection, identifies a balance of menu items in each category of the menu that offers the customer a blend of texture, taste, and colour. These items also fulfil the requirements of production, service, and cost that management must consider in order to operate a successful restaurant.

Standards

Standards are the measures of performance that management sets in order to establish objectives that can help to achieve the overall goals of the business. In food production those standards are

1. Standard recipe card
2. Standard cost card

3. Standard purchasing specification
4. Standard portion
5. Standard plate presentation

If the established standards are met in all five areas, the objectives of high-quality food production and established food cost percentages will be attained. When any one or more of these standards are not met, the objectives for the entire menu program are jeopardized. If, for example, the portion size of a menu item is arbitrarily changed in food production by the use of the wrong size serving spoon, food costs will increase.

This will now set off a chain reaction that results in an increased food cost percentage for this menu item. At the same time the kitchen is mistakenly using an 8-ounce boned chicken breast instead of a 6-ounce portion. As chicken is costing $0.14 per ounce, the food cost on this item has just increased by $0.28. The customers will also expect that menu item to be served with the same size chicken breast the next time that they order it. The server will have to overcome this expectation created by the improper portioning of food product.

Menu pricing is a management skill that requires a thorough knowledge of an operations costs and profit goals and a realistic appraisal of what the market (customer) will bear in menu prices. Profit in a restaurant operation is generated by revenues. Revenues are produced directly by sales of menu items.

Menu item pricing is based on four pricing formats in which the menu may be presented. These four formats place menu items together in pricing groupings. Management must establish the general pricing format to be used to establish an average check. Four components of pricing must be considered in order to achieve menu prices that accurately reflect the needs of the operation in order to produce a desired profit for owners and investors:

1. Food cost
2. Labour cost
3. Overhead cost
4. Profit

These four elements of the pricing structure together represent 100 percent of the selling price. Pricing formulas are a series of mathematical equations that offer management a variety of options as to how they price menu items. Each formula represents a technique of food service accounting and reflects a different theory of restaurant management.

Menus have traditionally been priced according to four basic formats. The initial pricing structure was termed d la carte, or "from the carte," the bill of fare or listing of what was being served for the day. On an a la carte menu every item is priced separately. With the advent of hotels and hotel dining rooms, the table d'hote, or "table of the hotel," system originated, offering one price for a full meal. From both of these pricing formats arose the need for variations, semi A la carte and semi table d'hote. The four formats are the following:

1. *A la carte*: all menu items are priced separately.
2. *Semi a la carte*: menu items are priced separately in most areas of the menu and grouped together in others.
3. *Table d'hote*: all menu items offered for a meal service are included in one price. This is often called prix fixe, French for "fixed price."

4. *Semi table d'hote*: menu items are grouped under one price in some areas of the menu and priced separately in others.

Menu pricing requires the application of marketing as well as accounting skills. Marketing skills are those techniques that help to promote the sale of the item. Accounting skills are those methods used in establishing a cost for the product and determining the selling price on the basis of the desired food cost percentage. Before determining a final menu price the following factors should be established:

1. What is the competition charging for the same or a similar menu item? Same or similar means that the same portion size that you are planning for is being served.

Men competitors' prices are reviewed, it is important that whoever is carrying out this function determine exactly what is included in the price. Does the price include an accompaniment such as franchises, lettuce and tomato, and/or vegetables? The price must be evaluated on the basis of the additional items. Portion sizes must also be approximately the same in order for a price comparison to have any value. For example, the competition is selling a fried shrimp item that includes six number 16 shrimp while your item includes six number shrimp.

2. How important is this menu item to your menu mix? Is this item a loser or a leader? Will higher volume sales allow the menu price to be lower and still create a profit?

The menu mix is the ranking of menu items in each category of the menu by sales volume and contribution to profit. A menu item with a high sales volume may not necessarily contribute to overall profit. On the contrary, it may be draining profit, depending on its food cost percentage and sales price. Items that both contribute to profit and have a high sales volume are called leaders. Items that have a low sales volume and do not contribute to profit are called losers. There are also items which have a highfood cost and high volume sales as well as those which have a lowfood cost and low volume sales.

Management will need to set a balance among these factors. The total menu is reviewed for the overall effectiveness of the pricing of all of the items.

3. What will the market (customer) bear as a price that reflects the perceived value of the item?

Determining what the market will bear is a marketing technique that requires evaluating the past history of menu item sales for an ongoing restaurant. It also requires an accurate analysis and assessment of the competition's volume sales of these items. Using a review of competitors' prices as a basis for pricing is only valid if all of the factors are known. In this case, it is necessary to have a substantial estimate of item sales.

Customer price acceptability is also based on the perceived value of the product to the customer. For example, prime rib of beef has a higher perceived value for many customers than does broiled breast of chicken. Stuffed lobster tail has a higher perceived value than poached filet of founder.

Management must take perceived value into consideration in setting menu prices. If the price is above or below customers' perceived value, then they will not buy it. In some cases, management is able to establish a menu price that will create more profit than the actual price in terms of food cost percentage.

On other occasions, management will have to run a

lower food cost percentage than desired in order to respond to customer demand and offer the menu item.

4. Is the menu price of this item compatible with the menu prices for other items in that menu category?

Pricing on the overall menu must keep within a certain dollar amount range in all categories. Entree prices should be held to within an $8 to $10 range of least expensive to most expensive.

Men customers are offered too wide a range of menu prices, they are faced with a decision to buy in the lower or higher range of prices. The results are confusion and a tendency to select menu items in the lower price range. By limiting the range of prices, customers feel comfortable about buying at either end of the pricing scale.

Menu prices that are established must be valid for at least a 6-month period. Printing good-quality menus is expensive and requires that price changes be made as infrequently as possible.

Menu prices must include a percentage to cover increased costs between menu printings. With this increased percentage menu items will at first generate a higher profit margin that will level off over the life of the printed page. An important management key is that the increased cost percentage factor is built into the pricing structure so that profits will not become losses by the time management is ready to reprint the menu.

Menu pricing method

Depending on management's theory of food costing and the style of the restaurant operation, a variety of methods can be applied for determining a selling price for menu items:

1. Food cost percentage method
2. Actual cost method
3. Prime cost method
4. Contribution to profit method

Food cost percentage method

The food cost percentage method is based on the management theory that the cost of food used to produce the item represents an established percentage of the selling price. This method also allows management the flexibility to price menu items individually.

Menu categories such as appetizers and desserts are often priced at a different food cost percentage than main course items. In order to calculate the food cost percentage method, two out of three primary factors must be known for the menu item:

1. Cost of food
2. Selling price
3. Food cost percentage

When any two of these factors are known, one of three pricing formulas can be applied to calculate the third. These three formulas and their abbreviations are the following:

1. Food cost ÷ selling price = food cost %

   FC ÷ SP = FC%

2. Food cost ÷ food cost % = selling price

   FC ÷ FC% = SP

3. Selling price × food cost % = food cost

   SP × FC% = FC

For example:

The menu item shrimp scampi has a selling price of \$9.50 and a food cost of \$3.40. The application of formula 1 produces a food cost percentage of 0.357, or 36 percent:

(FC) \$3.40 + (SP) \$9.50 = (FC%) 36%

The menu item breast of chicken salad has a desired food cost percentage of 35 percent and a food cost of \$3.50. The application of formula 2 yields a selling price of \$10.00:

(FC) \$3.50 - (FC%) 35% = (SP) \$10.00

The menu item broiled crab cakes has a selling price of \$16.95 and a desired food cost percentage of 30 percent. The application of formula 3 finds \$5.08 available for food cost:

(SP) \$16.95 X (FC%) 30% = (FC) \$5.08

Menu items may need to be offered at a higher or lower food cost percentage in order to be made available as specials and promotional items. If the balance of the menu has been calculated to produce a predetermined food cost percentage, then the sales of items with a fluctuating food cost percentage should be averaged into the total costs.

The food cost percentage method has the advantage of being able to be calculated on a daily or even a per-food-service basis, if a computer food service system is used. Management can immediately spot food cost percentage variances in both individual items and total sales.

Actual cost method

The actual cost method is applied to situations in which management has already established the selling price and needs to determine what is available for the cost of food ingredients. The actual cost method establishes desired percentages of costs based on a profit goal. Desired revenues are calculated in terms of these figures. Table 1 outlines the actual cost method. In this example, the profit goal is set at 10 percent of total revenues.

Owners and investors have preestablished a profit goal of $250,000. If profit represents 10 percent of total revenues, then desired annual revenue becomes $2,500,000. Overhead and profit are calculated as $500,000 and $750,000, respectively, bringing the total of profit and costs to $1,450,000. When this figure is subtracted from total revenues, the balance available for food cost is $1,050,000. The result of the application of the food cost percentage formula Food Cost ÷ Sales = Food Cost % is a food cost percentage of 40 percent. The available food cost for each menu item is now calculated by applying the equation:

$$\text{Selling Price} \times \text{Food Cost \%} = \text{Food Cost}$$

Restaurants that often need to apply this method of costing are chain operations such as Bennigan's, TGI Friday's, and Chili's. The pricing range for each menu category is established by the corporate office. Company management has already set a pricing policy that requires actual menu prices to fall within certain dollar figures. For example; appetizer prices must be priced between $3.95 and $5.95. The menu prices are established on a regional basis and management must use these prices.

Table 1
Actual cost method

Estimated total food sales		$2,500,000
Profit goal		
10% Profit goal	250,000	
Estimated costs		

20% Overhead	500, 000	
30% Labour Cost	750,000	
Total:	1,500,000	–1,500,000
Available for food cost		$1,000,000
(FC) $1,550,000 ÷ (SP) $2,5000 = 40%		

Management, however, is also responsible for producing no more than a 40 percent food cost, regardless of problems with local distributors and price fluctuations. Management now applies the following calculations to each menu item to establish exactly how high the cost of food can be and still produce a 40 percent food cost.

Menu item	Menu price		FC%		Food cost
Caesar salad	$3.50	×	40%	=	$1.40
Broiled scallops	$10.75	×	40%	=	4.30
Chocolate mousse	$3.75	×	40%	=	1.50

Prime cost method

The prime cost method is applied to menu programs that use a large amount of preprepared food products as ingredients. As the availability and increasing costs of labour present greater concerns to restaurant operators, preprepared food items offer cost saving alternatives.

Table 2
Prime cost calculation

Menu Item	Portion Size	Raw	Preprepared	Labour Time	Labour Cost Recipe/pp
Clam chowder	20	×	25 min	25 min	3.25/17
Fried oysters	10	×	35 min	45 min	5.85/13
Chicken salad	15	×	15 min	25 min	3.25/.22
Crab cakes	10	×	30 min	40 min	3.90/.52

Food products that are preprepared in some form include in their costs the labour for that preproduction. As some portion of the labour cost required to complete the finished product is part of the cost of the food product, management should account for that cost in calculating the selling price. When 40 percent or more of food ingredients used in an operation fall into the category of preprepared, the prime cost method should be applied to achieve more accurate pricing.

Table 3
Prime cost pricing method

Menu Item	Food Cost +	Labour Cost =	Prime Cost × 2=	Menu Price
Clam chowder	0.24	0.17	0.41	0.82
Fried oysters	1.33	0.13	1.46	2.92
Chicken salad	1.12	0.22	1.34	2.68
Crab cakes	2.80	0.52	3.32	6.64

Prime cost method management begins by identifying every item on the ingredient list as either raw or preprepared. The labour time is calculated for each item, whether raw or preprepared, from the initial use of the product to final production. On the basis of hourly wage the labour time is given a value that now becomes the direct labour cost.

To establish a selling price, now calculate a pricing factor. The pricing factor is determined by dividing the percentage of cost into 100. Direct labour costs for a raw food product are generally calculated at 10 percent of the selling price. An established 40 percent food cost and the 10 percent direct labour cost total 50 percent. The next step is to divide 100 by 0.50 to find a factor of 2. The factor is now multiplied by the prime cost to calculate a menu price.

$$\text{Prime cost} \times \text{factor} = \text{menu price}$$

Table 3 illustrates the calculation of a selling price using this method.

Contribution to profit

The contribution to profit method is based on the

selection of menu prices according to what the customer will pay for an item and the contribution that the item sales will make to the gross profit of the operation. Each menu item is evaluated according to customer acceptability and projected sales volume. The initial selling price for each menu item is based on a desired food cost percentage as in the chart in Table 4. The final selling price is determined by management's estimation of what the customer will perceive as an acceptable selling price for that item

Example

1. An 8-ounce chicken breast stuffed with cheese and ham and surrounding items will have an actual food cost of $2.29. This item, when calculated at a 35 percent food cost, has a selling price of $6.54. Management feels that customers will accept a higher selling price of $9,25. At $9.25 the contribution to gross profit on this item is $6.96.

2. A 9-ounce slice of prime rib of beef with surrounding items has a food cost of $5.18 and a selling price of $12.95 with a 40 percent food cost. Management decides that they would like to encourage volume sales of prime ribs to create a promotional menu item to increase overall sales. Volume purchasing prices will also help to lower the food cost. The selling price is dropped to $8.65, which will produce a 60 percent food cost. The contribution to gross profit on this item is $3.47. Volume sales will, however, increase this amount. If the item were left at the higher sales price, there would be resistance to pricing, resulting in lower sales. Although the individual contribution to profit would be higher, the volume increase would not occur.

3. Ravioli crevette has a food cost of $4.55. Calculated at

a 33 percent food cost, the selling price of this item is $13.67. Management feels that this is a selling price that customers will find acceptable and adjusts the menu price to $13.95. The contribution to gross profit on this item is $9.40.

Table 4
Contribution to profit method

Item	Food Cost	(FC%)	Selling Price	Merit Price (MP)	Contribution to Gross Profit (GP)
A	$2.29	35	$6.54	$9.25	$6.96
B	$5.18	40	$12.95	$8.95	$3.77
C	$4.55	33	$13.67	$13.95	$9.40

Combined menu pricing methods

The four menu pricing methods discussed in this chapter can often be used in combination with one another depending on the type of food service operation and management's abilities to identify effective combinations and carry them out in daily operations. A combination of menu pricing methods is effectively developed to achieve managements' specific profit objectives by the Melrose Diner in the case study at the beginning of this chapter. Of the four pricing methods discussed in this section only the actual cost method is not applied by the management of the Melrose Diner. When profit goals and objectives are clearly stated and management is capable of effectively determining how to apply pricing methods to their operation, a combination of pricing methods can be successful.

Establishing selling prices that effectively meet the needs of an operation takes careful research and planning. Achieving the goals that these prices are calculated to meet requires daily monitoring of fluctuating food costs and food cost percentages. Listening to customers daily becomes an important part of reacting to their needs and demands. The production sheet, sales mix, and menu re-evaluation are control systems that keep management abreast of changes on a daily and a weekly basis.

Making a profit is the primary goal of any "for profit" business regardless of the service or the product offered. Non-profit businesses are community-service-oriented and must apply business techniques to break even, or create enough revenue to cover the costs incurred.

Profit can be defined as

1. The excess of returns over expenditures in a transaction or series of transactions
2. The excess of the selling price of goods and services over all related costs
3. Net after-tax income, usually for a given period

Profit feasibility is the predetermination by owners and managers of the probability for excess returns over expenditures. In order to determine profit feasibility it is necessary to outline all the operational activities of the planned business and estimate their individual costs and sales volumes. From these figures one can accurately calculate the feasibility of probable income and profits. In an ongoing operation this process is done by analysing the statement of income and expense. Calculating the break-even point for a restaurant business is one of the first steps in profit analysis.

The break-even point is that point in business operations where revenue equals cost. Anticipated profit can be projected from that point on. In establishing a new business operation it is necessary to follow the outline of a feasibility chart. In an ongoing operation this same chart should be developed to make sure that management is aware of the information necessary to establish the feasibility level of proposed profit goals accurately.

Cost is made up of three major segments:

1. Food cost
2. Labour cost
3. Overhead cost

Each of the three primary areas of cost has a major impact on the success of a restaurant business. Management should be aware of the profile of each area and how it can affect the overall profitability of the operation.

Direct and indirect costs

Costs are those expenses which are both direct and indirect expenses of operating a business. The general guideline for distinguishing costs is that direct costs are any expenses directly related to providing the product and/or service to the customer and are normally affected by volume, whereas indirect costs are those expenses which are necessary to maintain the operating business and are not affected by changes in the volume of business.

In addition, a subcategory of direct costs breaks out the major expenses entailed in the direct production and service of the product. The following listing identifies the various expense areas of direct and indirect costs:

Direct operating expenses

a. Linen, china, glass, and flowers

b. Costs of cleaning and associated supplies

c. Employee uniforms and laundry costs

d. Cooking equipment, utensils, and kitchen tools
e. Restaurant decorations, including flowers
f. Menus, wine lists, and other promotional material
g. Licenses and permits

Utility expenses

a. Heat, light and power, including any type of energy use (gas, oil, electricity, and other canned or bottled fuel used in restaurants)
b. Water, ice, and trash removal

Administrative expenses

Costs directly related to the operation of the business management of the restaurant, including

a. Telephone services and equipment rental
b. Computer and data-processing costs
c. Office supplies and printed materials used in the business management of the operation
d. Insurance costs not related to either employee benefits or building occupation costs
e. Management fees, such as accountanting and property management
f. Security services
g. Professional dues and expenses

Advertising expenses: promotional costs, including

a. Advertising through any of the media
b. Costs of advertising or public relations agencies

Repairs and maintenance expenses: costs associated with the physical maintenance of the restaurant property, including

a. Interior or exterior design costs

b. Maintenance of furniture, upholstery, and window hangings

c. Repairs to furnishings, floor coverings, and building structure

d. Repairs to refrigeration, air conditioning, plumbing, heating, kitchen and dishwashing and sanitation equipment

Occupation expenses: expenses that do not change regardless of the volume of the restaurant's business

Primary areas of costs

Primary costs are the expenses for labour and the purchase of food and beverages. The following are the three primary cost areas:

1. Food cost: direct costs related to the purchase of any food-related product used in a restaurant
2. Beverage cost: direct costs related to the purchase of any beverage-related product, alcoholic or non-alcoholic, used in a restaurant
3. Labour cost
    a. Wages and salaries, including vacation pay, overtime, commissions, and bonuses paid to employees
    b. Costs of the following employee benefits

       Social Security

       Federal and state unemployment taxes

       State health insurance tax

       Workmen's Compensation insurance premiums

       Welfare payment plans

Pension plans

Insurance for health, accident, hospitalization, Blue Cross, Blue Shield, and other group policy premiums

Expenses directly related to the well-being of the employee, such as meals, transportation, education, and employee activities

Managing these costs requires that standards for purchasing as well as specific procedures for receiving, distribution, billing, and accountability be established throughout an operation. The margin for error between breaking even and making a profit in today's highly competitive and high cost market is minimal. Management's ability to recognize fluctuations and overruns in all areas of cost is essential to the success of any business in the 1990s.

Statement of income and expenses

Before investors, owners, and managers can attempt to determine profit feasibility for a new or ongoing operation it is necessary that they outline all of these costs in an organized manner. The statement of income and expense in Table 1 was developed by the National Restaurant Association in cooperation with the hospitality accounting firm of Laventhol and Horwath as a guide for restaurateurs, offering sales and expense terminology that applies directly to their businesses.

When accurate information is used to complete the form, feasible and/or accurate profitability can be calculated. The dollar figures are also translated into percentages of cost and income. This format breaks down expenses into manageable areas of accounting which are often more relevant to restaurant managers than traditional accounting terminology.

Expenses are direct or indirect, depending on their relationship to the production of the product and/or service.

In this worksheet the assignment of costs to one category or another goes a step further by designating some expenses as either controllable costs or occupation costs. This further designation allows management to identify costs that might possibly be decreased. Controllable costs are the following:

— Payroll

— Employee benefits

— Direct operating expenses

— Music and entertainment

— Advertising and promotion

— Utilities

— Administrative and general

— Repairs and maintenance

The labour costs listed under primary costs, itemize the breakdown of costs that are included in both payroll and employee benefits. Other primary cost areas are itemized under expense categories, such as direct operating expense, utility expense, administrative expense, advertising expense, and repairs and maintenance expense.

Occupation costs are the following:

— Rent

— Property taxes

— Other taxes

— Property insurance

Additional information required on this worksheet is listed under supplemental operating information as

Sales per seat

Food $

Beverage $

Average receipt (check) per seat $

Daily seat turnover (turnover rate)

This information is needed to develop a feasibility chart which is the basis for profit analysis accurately.

A comparison of this information with the statement presented in Table 1 gives a more concise picture of the distribution of costs and expenses of the average restaurant surveyed. Profit in this chart is designated as net income before income taxes.

To identify areas of cost that resulted in a net loss for La Brasserie and La Belle, Inc., each area of cost on the statement of income and expense must be analysed. Profiles of the areas where La Brasserie and La Belle, Inc., costs ran over industry norms are apparent. Management can investigate these areas to determine the changes necessary to decrease costs and increase profits.

Feasibility chart

Before establishing the probability of profit it is necessary to outline all of the operational activities of a restaurant business. This can be done by using the format in Table 3-6. If a statement of income and expense has been developed, total amounts for operating costs can be entered on the feasibility chart. In this example, total operating costs have been estimated at $1,000,000. Using a desired gross profit percentage of 20 percent, the calculated profit margin ($200,000) can be entered along with total sales needed, in order to cover both costs and profit goals.

Table 1
Feasibility chart

Total estimated operating costs for one year:	1,000, 000, 00
20% of total costs as calculated profit margin:	200,000.00
Total sales needed to cover costs and profit:	2,000,000.00
Restaurant Statistics	
Number of meal services:	2
Anticipated seating turnover	
Lunch:	2.5
Dinner:	1.5
Seating Capacity: 250	
Number of days open annually: 307	
Total number of customers served daily: 1,000	
Adjusted average number of customers served daily, based on projected 75% occupancy:	750
Total estimated number of customers served annually, based on 75 % occupancy:	230,250
Average lunch check:	$6.00
Daily lunch revenue:	469 X 6.00 = $2,814
Average dinner check:	$15.50
Daily dinner revenue:	281 X 15.50 = $4,355.50
Daily lunch and dinner revenue:	$7,169.50
Total estimated annual revenue:	$2,201,036.50
Total sales needed:	$2,000,000.00

Management now lists the known restaurant statistics and determines a realistic percentage of occupancy for a 1-year period. In an ongoing operation this percentage can be developed by referring to past sales history. The average check information is established for a new operation by using the current menu prices of the direct competition as a guideline. To find the average check amount that customers must spend in order to produce enough income to cover the costs and anticipated profits, divide the number of customers annually into the combined costs and desired profit totals.

Total annual costs	2,000,000
20 percent gross profit	200,000
Total:	2,200,000
Total customers annually	230,250

2,200,000 - 230,250 = $9.55 (average check).

Once the average checks have been determined, daily meal service revenues can be multiplied by anticipated customer counts (ACC) to find daily revenue totals.

Average lunch check

Daily lunch revenue: × ACC = $ Lunch Period Revenue Total

Average dinner check

Daily dinner revenue: × ACC = $ Dinner Period Revenue Total.

Daily lunch and dinner revenue: $ Daily Revenue Total.

These figures are then multiplied by the number of days open to determine probable annual revenue figures. This figure is now compared to the total sales needed to cover both costs and profit.

Total estimated annual revenue: $

Total sales needed: $

The application of the break-even point can be used by management as an additional tool by which to judge feasibility:

Total estimated annual revenue: $

Total sales needed: $

Breakeven point: $

The feasibility of this operation is determined by whether

or not enough sales can be generated to cover costs and desired profit. In this example, estimated sales exceed the amount needed by a specific amount. This indicates that if the income and expenses hold true and the figures used to calculate percentage of occupancy and average checks are accurate, this operation can produce a feasible profit for investors and owners.

In addition, enough sales are possible above those needed to ensure a safety cushion against changes in the numbers in those areas which can directly affect revenues. The decision as to whether a restaurant business is feasible is significantly different from the decision that profit is feasible.

Profit goals

The profit goals owners and managers establish must be based on an accurate assessment of the feasibility of the operation and include an analysis of profit percentages from operations in the same category of restaurant operation. These dollar figures and percentages represent restaurant operations classified into lower (quick service), median (casual-family style), and upper (full service). Actual dollar profit is calculated per seat. Dollar profit is converted to the percentage of total sales that it represents. Comparing both the dollar profit and the percentage of each category yields the following conclusions:

1. Full-service style generates more income per seat.
2. Casual-family style generates approximately one-third of the income per seat that full service does.
3. Quick-serve generates less dollar profit per seat but higher volume profit.

A quick overview of this analysis might lead to the assumption that full-service restaurants are more profitable than quick serve. This assumption is proved incorrect, however, when the percentages of profit are multiplied first by the actual profit dollar and then by the percentage of seat occupancy:

Purchase × % Profit = Total Sales = % Seat Occ

\$ 52 × 1.4% = \$ 728.00 × 75% = \$5,460.00

\$368 × 9.2% = \$ 3,385.60 × 50% = \$16,928.00

\$945 × 19.4% = \$18,333.00 × 35% = \$6,416.55

Guidelines for gross profit margins range widely from 4 percent for quick serve to 20 percent for ambitious full-service restaurants as industry standards.

5

Employee Organisation

Food service position

In order to understand the type of job positions available in most food service businesses, it is helpful to look at the job descriptions and organizational charts of restaurants and kitchens. Restaurant operations require a total food service management team. Whether part of a hotel/ resort or a restaurant chain or controlled by independent ownership, restaurants generally have the same type of organizational chart. The number of job positions in each category will depend on the size of the restaurant and the volume of business.

Front of the house positions

Restaurant manager: In an independent restaurant operation the restaurant manager works in conjunction with the chef while maintaining total authority and responsibility for the entire operation. Staffing and training are a major function of this position along with handling guest relations.

In addition, the manager is responsible for the profitability of the operation. This involves determining food and beverage costs as well as pricing and developing the menu program. The condition of the building and surrounding property as well as the safety and sanitation practices of the operation are also major responsibilities.

In a situation where there are multiple restaurants and individual managers for each unit, many of these responsibilities will be taken over by purchasing managers, house engineers, food and beverage managers, and controllers.

Assistant manager: In an independent restaurant the assistant manager is often assigned some of the responsibilities of the manager. The assistant manager is responsible for the entire operation in the absence of the manager. In many operations the assistant manager assumes responsibility for training front of the house staff. In a multiunit facility the assistant manager is often the maitre d'hotel.

Dining room captains: The responsibility for service and guest relations within identified sections of the dining room, known as stations, during assigned service times is the primary function of this position. Dining room captains should have a good working knowledge of table side food preparations and be able to train other staff members. To take full advantage of this position a good knowledge of the wine list and menu is important.

Wait staff and bus persons: These positions are responsible for providing high-quality, professional service to guests in a friendly manner. The style of restaurant operation will identify the type of service that wait staff must be able to provide. Bus persons assist wait staff when necessary and are responsible for clearing between courses and resetting the table.

Hosts and hostesses: These positions are responsible for greeting customers, assigning seating, and backing up the wait staff whenever possible. Full service restaurants often employ a maitre'd for this position, depending on the level of formality of atmosphere and service. Casual family-style operations generally employ a host or hostess for these duties.

Head bartender: In restaurant operations with more than one alcoholic beverage outlet the head bartender is responsible for purchasing, staffing, training, and overseeing beverage costs. Bartenders, cocktail servers, and cashiers report to the head bartender.

Back of the house positions

Executive chef: The responsibilities of the executive chef vary according to the type and size of food service operation. In a hotel facility the executive chef can manage up to four or five kitchens depending on the size of the overall facility and volume of food service related business. He or she may also supervise a number of assistant chefs (sous chefs) who are assigned to the kitchens of various food service outlets. A knowledge of the application of computer food service programs is essential in a position of this magnitude.

In a freestanding restaurant seating approximately 250 guests the executive chef often becomes the purchasing agent as well as working on the production line.

Assistant executive chef (*Sous chef*): The assistant executive chef is often called by the French term for this kitchen position, sous chef. The sous, chef's responsibilities include being able to assume any of the line cook positions as well as to assume responsibility for the kitchen in the absence of the executive chef.

Line cooks: Line cooks are assigned to various cooking stations in the kitchen. The size of the kitchen facility and variety of cooking methods used for preparation will determine the number of stations on the cooking line. The grill station, saute station, and broiler station are features of many kitchens. Some line cooks specialize in a particular area of food preparation, such as garde manger work.

Cold food displays, salad and buffet preparations, as well as ice sculptures are usually within the preparation capabilities of a garde manger chef.

Pastry chef: Pastry chefs are primarily responsible for the production of desserts rather than breads and rolls. Often, a pastry chef will become involved with highly creative display pieces for buffets and decoration. This particular area of food preparation is expected to be in greater demand by industry in the 1990s than any other. It is estimated that the need for pastry chefs and bakers will increase by 35 percent by the year 2000.

A large hotel/ resort complex generally operates at least three food service outlets.

Quick-serve operations

The job descriptions for positions in quick serve operations are a blend of front and back of the house functions. The close proximity of the customer to food production stations requires a different system of allocating management responsibilities than often exists in a full service restaurant. The following job descriptions are common to store positions in most of the major quick serve restaurant chains.

Quick serve restaurant job descriptions

Store manager: The manager, like any other restaurant manager, is responsible for overseeing the entire operation, including sales volume and profitability. Because of the 24-hour operations schedule of many quick serve operations, this position requires the ability to handle a diverse group of employees, often in a multilingual setting.

First assistant: The first assistant actively administers the crew training program. Responsibilities of this position include monthly budget projections and all personnel functions for the store.

Second assistant: The second assistant must be capable of operating the store. This position also requires the ability to conduct personnel interviews.

Swing manager: The swing manager runs assigned shifts of the store operation, directing the crew and dealing with customers.

Swing trainee: The swing trainee assists in managing the store in preparation for promotion to the position of swing manager.

Crew leader: The crew leader is responsible for assigned areas of the store during the shift. A positive teamwork attitude and the ability to communicate that to other crew members are essential to this position.

Crew trainer: The crew trainer is responsible for training all new hires. Leadership ability and good people handling skills are necessary for this position.

Crew person:The crew person is responsible for carrying out the activities of the area of the restaurant to which he or she is assigned.

Job descriptions

A job description lists the duties and responsibilities of a position that has been formally established in an organization. Every position listed on an organization chart should have a corresponding job description. By going through the exercise of creating an organization chart and corresponding job descriptions, management forms a much clearer picture of their organization.

Lines of authority, communication, responsibility, promotion, and work are specified so that areas that have been characterized by inconsistency, miscommunication, and low productivity can be identified. Often, management recognizes areas where authority is overlapping, causing confusion and often hostility among the staff.

The line of work that has become tangled because of confusion regarding job responsibility can now be set out for the more effective accomplishment of work. Communication is a vital linking pin in any successful business. When managers and staff are unsure of exactly who is responsible for job functions and who has authority over whom, communications become ineffective. Individual job descriptions clearly identify authority and responsibility, giving both managers and staff an accurate understanding of the job.

Successful training programs integrate visual aids with hands on application, reinforcement and continued management supervision. Well designed and systematically implemented training programs decrease costs and increase profitability.

Hiring, training, retaining, and firing employees are key management functions representing a major cost to any business operation. Employees are a significant part of overall operating costs. In addition to the hourly wage or salary, employers can expect to add 25 percent to an employee's pay as the cost of benefits. The operational costs of hiring, training, and firing can average as much as an additional $600.00 per employee.

Good interview skills improve the quality of the hiring practices of an organization. The ability to access an applicant's attitudes and personality accurately can help to identify potential employees for designated job positions.

When the right person is hired for the right job, the employee performs to the employer's expectations. Satisfied employees stay in job positions, absorb training, become part of a team, and contribute to an organization.

Training is an integral part of the continued success of a business. Well-developed training programs include job orientation, instruction, evaluations, and development training. Employees who are continually given the initiative and skills to take on new and better paying positions stay and grow within an organization.

Hiring

Hiring employees for designated positions is the final step in a selection process that begins with a recognized need for labour. This labour shortage can be generated by a vacancy created by the loss of an employee or a growing demand for employees.

Recruiting

The method applied to recruit new employees is dependent on the level of the job position to be filled. Worker and staff positions are usually posted in the personnel office or appropriate locations in an operation. They are also listed in the classified Help Wanted section of local newspapers.

The Equal Employment Opportunity Commission and the Fair Employment Practices Commission have laid down strict guidelines that must be followed in the announcement of the availability of any job position.

Employment agencies and advertisements in appropriate newspapers and trade journals are used to recruit employees for middle and upper management positions.

Large food service companies have professional recruiters on staff who visit schools and colleges and other sources of employees, conducting formal recruiting programs. To interest prospective applicants, companies issue recruitment announcements and job descriptions that outline the job opportunity and benefits.

The applications generated by these recruiting

efforts form the applicant pool from which management can identify job candidates. For middle and upper management level positions resumes are also submitted with applications.

Resumes provide a detailed breakdown of an applicant's employment history as well as information about education, professional associations, and achievements. Having determined a set of criteria or guidelines for the position, management selects for interviews those applicants who qualify to the extent that they would like to assess their attitudes, personality, and personal characteristics.

Interview

The interview process allows the employer to assess prospective employees on a one to one basis. There are two basic interview formats known, the direct interview and the indirect interview.

Direct Interview: The direct interview is a highly structured situation with preplanned questions asked of the candidate in a set pattern. These questions have been designed to elicit specific information regarding experience, capabilities, and other factors that the employer feels are necessary to indicate the eligibility of the candidate.

Indirect Interview: The indirect interview combines a planned format with a flexible question and answer scenario. Questions are designed so that the candidate can respond more spontaneously, often revealing personality traits and attitudes.

Interview questions

Managers who are developing interview questions should be aware of what they may and may not ask a prospective employee under the laws and guidelines set down by federal anti-discrimination laws. The following are general guidelines concerning information that an interviewer may not attempt to elicit in an interview. The interviewer may not ask questions in the following categories to which the applicant must supply information which will reveal the information indicated:

— *Name*: National origin, marital status or original name if applicant has legally changed his or her name.

— *Birthplace*: Birthplace of applicant or applicant's parents.

— *Religion*: Applicant's religious preference or affiliation as well as what church or parish is attended and religious holidays observed.

— *Age*: Age, or date of birth except where such information is necessary in order to satisfy state or local laws as well as guidelines governing apprenticeship programs and employee benefit programs.

— *Sex*: Sex, marital status or number of dependents of the applicant.

— *Race or colour*: Applicant's race or skin colour.

— *Marital status*: Whether an applicant is single, divorced, married or widowed as well as the number of children.

— *Education*: Applicant's race, nationality or religious preference.

— *Citizenship*: Applicant and applicant's families citizenship or date of U.S. citizenship or status of naturalization.

— *Military record*: Draft classification or eligibility for military service or date and conditions of discharge.

— *Arrest record*: Arrest record unless directly related to the responsibilities of the job.

— *Handicaps*: Whether a handicap exists and the extent of that handicap.

The content of interview questions is determined by the type of information that the interviewer needs to evaluate the applicant. Some job positions require direct questions relating to job experience, training, and skill level. The interviewer will also ask questions that can reveal how the applicant works with others.

Middle and upper level management job positions require more indirect questions aimed at assessing the applicant's personal characteristics, personnel and attitudes as well as technical information. Applications and resumes for these positions have already provided in-depth work experience, education, and training information.

Guidelines for job orientation

1. Present a complete job description for the position.
2. Outline each specific job task for the position.
3. Divide each job task into a series to instructional steps.
4. Establish a training method for each instructional step.
5. Determine the amount of time for each instructional step.
6. With the employee, establish a training schedule for each instructional step.
7. Execute the first instructional step using the designated training method.
8. Evaluate the employee's job performance.

9. Proceed to the second instructional step only when both you and the employee are satisfied that the task can be completed successfully.

Law in the workplace

The most recent of these laws, the American Disabilities Act (ADA), protects the rights of individuals with disabilities. These protections include hiring practices as well as the ability of disabled persons to function within the workplace. Because a restaurant requires a variety of physical activities to be performed in many job positions and good communications skills in others, understanding of the requirements of this law is important for managers at every level of an operation.

Employers will be required to recognize a prospective employee's disability and how that disability may or may not limit his or her ability to perform specific job tasks related to job positions. The ADA defines the term disability as follows:

— An impairment that substantially limits one or more major life activities, such as walking, hearing, speaking, seeing, learning, or working

— A record of an impairment that substantially limits major life activities from which the individual is recovering or has recovered

— An assumption by others that an impairment exists which in actuality does not, such as the presence of hearing aids and severe scarring from accidents or burns

The American Disabilities Act: Questions and Answers (Washington, D.C.) p. 2, Office on the Americans with Disabilities Act, U.S. Department of justice, states that an employer may not discriminate against a qualified disabled person who can perform the necessary functions of a job position:

> A qualified individual with a disability is a person who meets legitimate skill, experience, education, or other requirements of an employment position that he or she holds or seeks, and who can perform the "essential functions" with or without reasonable accommodation. If the individual is qualified to perform essential job functions except for limitations caused by the disability; the employer must consider whether the individual could perform these functions with a reasonable accommodation. If a written job description has been prepared in advance of advertising or interviewing applicants for a job, this will be considered as evidence, although not necessarily conclusive evidence, of the essential functions of the job.

Reasonable accommodation includes making existing facilities accessible to and usable by disabled employees, changing specific job functions, adapting equipment, or modifying educational programs and training materials. Under this act, accommodation must also be made to allow any disabled person to enjoy goods and services in public accommodations fully and equally.

Employers are required to meet the following specific requirements in their job hiring, training, and firing practices:

— Reasonably accommodate the disabilities of qualified applicants or employees unless to do so will cause undue hardship.

— Not discriminate against a qualified individual with a disability simply because they do not want to make reasonable accommodations.

— Not use employment tests to screen out people with disabilities unless the tests or criteria are job-related and consistent with business necessity

— Make only those preemployment inquiries concerning medical conditions that are strictly job-related.

— Not require preemployment medical exams. Conditional offers of employment may be made pending the results of medical exams if all new employees must have such exams, An applicant may not be rejected because of medical exam results unless the reasons for rejection are job-related and consistent with business necessity.

— Not discriminate against a qualified individual because of a known relationship or association with an individual with a disability.

Employers are given specific rights under the Americans with Disabilities Act:

— To counter discrimination charges by proving that the alleged discriminatory standards are job-related and consistent with business necessity and that the worker could not have done the job without reasonable accommodation.

— To reject applicants or fire employees who pose a significant risk to the health and safety of other individuals in the workplace.

— To use traditional risk assessment considerations when designing health benefit plans. Some restrictions do apply to this area.

In job interviews employers may not ask the following questions which relate to disabilities:

1. Whether a prospective employee has a disability.
2. Whether a prospective employee has a physical problem limiting his or her ability to carry out specific job tasks.
3. Whether a person has a history of drug or alcohol abuse.

4. Whether a person has filed for worker compensation claims and on what basis.
5. Whether there is a history of health problems.

Interview questions in these areas should be focused on the prospective employee's ability to perform specific job tasks. Managers should be particularly sensitive to this act and make every effort to be fully knowledgable about accommodations that must be made to an operation's physical facilities as well as employee practices.

The Americans with Disabilities Act is legislation that recognizes the contributions that persons with disabilities can make to the workplace as both employees and customers, restricting the ability of both employers and operators of public accommodations to prejudge their abilities to perform, participate, and enjoy.

Job orientation

Once the position has been offered to an applicant and accepted, the most important stage in the hiring process, job orientation, must take place.

To train an employee effectively, it is necessary for management to state the tasks and responsibilities of the job position clearly in a job specification or analysis. These guidelines assure that management knows exactly what functions the worker will serve. After presenting and discussing these specifications with the employee, job instruction begins.

Instructions for each position should be developed to establish a standard orientation to the job as well as to allow management to assess the skills and abilities of new employees.

Often, worker and staff positions employ the buddy system, pairing the trainee with an experienced worker who carries out the same job effectively. This system can be a direct introduction to the job or a method for reinforcing training.

Training

Training is a management skill which is most effective when a variety of training techniques and methods are applied in a wide range of situations. Effective trainers must have the capacity to listen as well as to instruct. There are established training methods that can be adapted to achieve an organization's training goals for individual positions. Management's training goals will change at each level of job authority and responsibility.

Worker level

At the worker level management's overall goal is to produce an established quality of product or service in a harmonious setting. Training is primarily task oriented with an emphasis on team compatibility if the task is to be completed by a group.

Staff level

The staff level positions often require a leadership role as either a crew leader, foreman, or supervisor. In addition to job task orientation, training methods are employed to teach management skills in group dynamics and leadership. Effective training methods provide role playing situations in which prospective managers learn how to react and interact with workers.

Middle management

The middle manager enters his or her position with the required skills and training to carry out a large portion of the job's responsibilities. Job orientation for this management level requires a thorough indoctrination program into the organization's goals, history, policies, expectations, and benefits. Organizational systems will have to be explained as well as standard operating procedures that affect the job position. Training for these positions is ongoing as an integral part of the job. Middle-level managers should consistently be exposed to training programs that will increase their effectiveness as leaders and coworkers. Training is also necessary to keep middle-level managers current on changes in techniques, developments, and advancements in their area of business.

Upper-level management

New employees in upper-level management positions follow the same orientation pattern as middle-level managers. The depth of their orientation into company goals and policies will depend on the impact that their decisions have on the future success of the business.

Training cycle

All training programs are developed in a series of steps that, when completed, lead to the next level of training for the employee. Effective training programs are ongoing, helping employees to learn new skills that will help them to advance into better paying job positions. The following outline details the training cycle:

Planning

1. The goals and objectives of any training activity must be clearly stated.

2. The amount of time needed for each segment of the training activity must be predetermined so that scheduling will not interfere with ongoing operations.

3. The teaching methods that are to be applied to the training activity must be established. Audiovisual equipment needs, handouts, workbooks, and evaluation procedures must be determined.

Preparation

1. The trainer is required to prepare the training area effectively so that the objectives of the training method can be accomplished. Materials and audiovisual equipment should be in place and working properly.

Presentation

1. The presentation of a training activity should be conducted within the established period.
2. The training period should be broken down into time segments. Each of these segments is assigned a presentation method that will hold the trainee's attention, create interest, and effectively instruct.

The presentation format should always allow for the flexibility of question and answer sessions at appropriate times in the program.

Application

1. Hands-on training allows the trainee to perform the task or activity covered in the training program. It is advisable that hands-on training take place in conjunction with formal training discussion.
2. The buddy system can be integrated into this segment of the training program. Working along with an experienced employee, the trainee can be directly instructed on a one-to-one basis.

Evaluation

1. Evaluation should be made at every stage of the training process. Written and oral quizzes will reinforce material in the presentation phase of the training program. Application can be evaluated at scheduled intervals as the employee gains confidence as well as ability to carry out the job task.

Training programs

Training programs are based on management objectives regarding the individual position. Worker and staff positions often have a high turnover rate which makes an investment in lengthy training programs too expensive to be cost-effective for the overall operation.

Training programs for such positions often have the short-range goal of getting the trainee out on the production line and effectively turning out the product or service required.

The problem with short-range training objectives is that they do not include the time to provide incentives to the trainee to learn new skills and continue into higher paying positions. This can often be accomplished by establishing incentive training goals that give employees incentive to learn new skills.

Long-range training programs have the advantage of being able to develop a plan to present skill development and information programs at scheduled times over a specific period. Initial training includes job orientation and training for the job position. Secondary training reinforces initial training and provides developmental skills and/or management techniques, depending on the position.

The financial benefits of job advancement by learning new skills and work methods give employees the incentive to

1. Maintain job interest, reducing absenteeism and labour turnover
2. Improve the overall quality of the product or service through their own performance
3. Develop company loyalty and retain their association with the company over a period of years.

Training methods

The application of a specific training method to a training program is dependent on the level of job positions included in the training session and a determination of short- or long-range goals for the skills being addressed, Training programs are generally classified as task-oriented or group and lecture.

Task-oriented training provides application of the job task as part of the direct training. In the application stage of the schedule the employee performs the job in conjunction with the training discussion. The buddy system or monitoring provides reinforced task application during actual job performance.

In group and lecture training the trainer communicates the information to a group of individuals in a passive setting where there is little or no opportunity for job application. There are, however, programs which provide the opportunity for role playing situations where managers are trained in employee management techniques and methods.

6

Front Office Management

Successful Front Office Management (FOMs) will ideally possess demonstrated competencies in both the oral and written communications they will need to deal with the complexities that exist among and between the three contexts of the model reproduced here. The FOM, therefore, becomes not only a manager and a communicator among and between the front office staff, the hotel departments and the guests, but also emerges as a communicator in yet another way—as a teacher and trainer.

This contextual theme of communications is carried forward in the essay contributed by James Bardi. Bardi further discusses the job of FOM, providing insights about the complexities of this job relative to not only communication but also to elements of an FOM job analysis, intrahotel relations, and the emerging and popular concept of employee empowerment.

A positive aspect of being the hub of a modem hotel for the front office staff is that it is keenly aware of what is happening at virtually every level of the hotel's organizational structure. One negative aspect is that the front office also serves as a lightning rod for guest complaints. This can be one of the most difficult things for the front office staff to learn to deal with, especially with the frequency and sometimes intensity of such complaints. Here again is an opportunity for FOMs, through staff training and empowerment, to utilize the power of their communications role to the advantage of both sides of the issue.

One major source of complaints related to the front office has to do with the accuracy of guest reservations and the attendant details. Honouring reservations in these days of lightning-fast communications and swift changes in plans can sometimes be problematic for not only the hotel but for the guest.

Hotels expect guests to honour their commitments to reservations and sometimes go to great lengths to secure guarantees through deposits or credit card commitments. Similarly, guests expect hotels to honour those commitments.

When these commitments are broken, the complaints discussed in the articles to come can be generated. Sometimes these complaints, depending on their magnitude and nature, can trigger lawsuits. Rutherford and McConnell discuss and analyse how hotels treat reservations, particularly if they have legal standing as a contract.

A companion article by Lambert, Lambert, and Cullen looks at the theoretical variables involved in the whole question of overbooking. Hotels know that a certain percentage of guests holding reservations won't show up; hotel FOMs know that a certain percentage of the hotel's current guests will stay over unexpectedly; a certain percentage of guests will check out early; a certain percentage of rooms will be out of order; and a multitude of other factors will affect the rate at which walk-ins arrive. Juggling all these variables is a job that's central to the task of the FOM, and Lambert and her colleagues discuss how this question may be attacked in a systematic way.

A former FOM who has moved on to top management once said that his job boiled down to the shortest job description in the hotel: "Fill the hotel; don't walk any guests."

All the challenges implicit in this simple statement make the hotel FOM's job a particularly difficult one. The legal implications of reservations and the hotel's need to maximize capacity lend complexity to the job of FOM, and the two articles introduced above should give the reader additional insights into those complexities.

Everyone who learned as a new desk clerk the meaning of the phrase "rack rate" also learned shortly thereafter that very few hotels ever achieve the ideal of renting rooms at rack rate on anything approaching a regular basis. The practice of discounting room rates is, therefore, nearly universal in the hotel industry.

The forces of business cycles, market segmentation, and other factors bear heavily on the way in which hotels respond to the issue of discounting, and the article here by Hanks, Cross, and Noland provides a window on the complexities of discounting while at the same time raising questions as to the extent to which FOMs and their staffs can participate in making decisions about pricing.

The questions raised here in theoretical form obviously play out for the FOM and his or her staff on a daily basis in the real world. This becomes particularly challenging when viewed in the context of the world's shortest job description.

Glenn Withiam, executive editor of *The Cornell Hotel and Restaurant Administration Quarterly,* contributes an essay updating his 1983 article on concierges, broadened to include an expanded realm of concierge services, their management and personnel. This article looks at how guest services are evolving as a significant and more truly integrated function of hotel service delivery than in the recent past when bell staffs, concierges, garage attendants, door people, and so forth, were something other than a seamless part of the organization.

Withiam looks at the concept of a professionalism paradigm for concierges in the 1990s and provides the reader with additional insights as to how these jobs enhance the transition of guests to the hotel and serve guests throughout their stay.

The theme of active communications carries forth throughout most of this section, particularly the topics of complaints, reservations, the intricacies of the FOM's job, and, increasingly, guest service.

The concluding article by Judi Brownell takes a broader look at the concept of the communications challenge by examining the entire realm of middle managers. Because the FOM is one of the first middle-management jobs most hotel professionals hold, the insights and concepts discussed by Brownell should be useful not only for potential FOMs but in other managerial contexts as well.

The articles presented here represent only a few of the range of issues attendant upon any modern hotel front office department. Duties, obligations, and responsibilities of front office personnel will change from hotel company to hotel company based on such variables as market segmentation, organizational structure, corporate philosophy, and individual leadership.

There is a great deal of management literature not specific to the front office but pertaining nonetheless to the various issues and challenges that face FOMs. The articles chosen for inclusion in this section are as specific as possible to the functional aspects of front office management. Other pertinent managerial insights may be applied from other contexts once the reader has a good functional grasp of the realm of front office activities. Included in the suggested readings are a number of specific textbooks that treat in great depth the functional and technical aspects of front office operations. What has been attempted here is an overview of pervasive managerial issues typical of those facing FOMs in the 1990s.

Front office personnel

While front offices may be organized in a number of different ways that depend on market segment, organizational or corporate philosophy, and practical or physical realities, the following job functions are normally found within the front office. This may vary, of course, from company to company.

These descriptions represent the editor's synthesis of personal experience, industry practices, and the work of the authors in the suggested readings. The books referenced there are outstanding, in-depth treatments of the intricacies of modem front office management and are widely used as texts and training aids.

The clerical staff that perform the reservation function handle a number of tasks that are important to the orderly accumulation and dissemination of reservation information to the departments that need it.

Reservation

The reservation staff handles guest communication and correspondence regarding reservations at the hotel. Contacts with potential guests can be in the form of mail, telephone, fax, electronic mail, telegraph, or a centralized computer reservation system. On the basis of this information, the staff creates and maintains reservation records for all advance reservations in the hotel. Once the information has been collected they produce and mail or otherwise communicate to the requester confirmations and/or guarantees.

As a part of reservations responsibilities, they track future room availability and may initiate forecasts of rooms sales and occupancy or produce other reservation-related statistics. Finally, on the day the guest is expected the reservation staff will "bring forward" reservations to the front office. This may be in the form of a physical reservation card or document or simply the release of that information in the hotel's data processing system.

In some hotel companies, the functions of reservations may be shifting to the marketing or sales department. This recognizes the importance of the sales department in producing group business and the close relationship that the sales staff and the reservations people must attain. By the same token, in other hotel organizations, the reservations function may remain in the front office, where it has historically been focused.

Cashier

As the name applies, cashiers deal with money in the maintenance and settling of guest accounts in the front office. Specifically, they are responsible for posting vouchers or charges that arrive during the day and evening shifts to guest accounts or the "city" ledger (credit accounts kept for individuals and businesses not guests of the hotel).

Cashiers are responsible for maintaining timely and accurate guest account folio balances. In most hotels the cashiers are the members of the front office staff who handle all cash transactions and checkouts of hotel guests at the front desk. They are responsible for settling guest accounts in whatever form payment is tendered: charge card, cash, check, or transfer to a master account.

It should be noted that in some smaller hotels the function of cashier is combined with that of room and/or reservation clerk because the size of the hotel demands it. In larger hotels, the cashier function is likely to be separate from other front office positions and may have several individuals fulfilling that role.

Night auditor

While night auditors typically work at the front desk, in an increasing number of hotels they report to the hotel controller as opposed to the front office manager. The fundamental role of the night auditor is to assure the hotel that departmental accounts and guest accounts are in balance at the close of the business day. To that end the night auditor posts charges and vouchers to guest accounts that are not posted by the day or evening cashiers, participates in routines that verify the accuracy and completeness of all guest accounts, and balances guest folio entries and departmental records.

A major portion of the night auditor's function is to post room and tax charges to guest accounts. Finally, the night auditor balances all accounts for the next day's business. A significant portion of the night auditor's task may involve tracking errors and discrepancies in room and departmental accounts; hence, the term "auditor."

Room clerks

The task of the room clerk may vary greatly from company to company and hotel to hotel. The size of the hotel, its market and its ambience are all elements that may affect the design and complexity of the room clerk's job. Suffice it to say, the room clerk is one of those positions whose focus at the front desk is very important to guest relations. Among the major responsibilities of the room clerk are assisting the guest in checking in. During this process, the clerk discusses with the guest the particular room rate most appropriate to that guest's wants and needs. This will vary with the type of accommodation the guest desires, the length of stay, and other requirements that are needed to register the guest.

The room clerk will then assist in the performance of the registration procedure, assign a room, determine the method of payment, and initiate the rooming process by dispensing and controlling keys and dispatching guest service staff to assist the guest to the room. The room clerk will report as necessary to front office management and is generally trained and expected by front office management to recognize and evaluate special situations and arrange for their attention. In many ways the room clerk is the eyes and ears of management regarding the operation of the hotel and its interface with the guest.

Front office assistant manager

The front office assistant manager supervises on a day-to-day basis all the operations and personnel of the front office. The front office assistant manager performs duties under the guidance and direction of the FOM. He or she is responsible for the smooth functioning of front office activities and processes and may work specifically with tour, group/convention, and/or corporate clients to help facilitate their access to the hotels and its services. The front office assistant manager will assist the FOM in hiring, staffing, scheduling, and training other front office personnel. A particular responsibility of this job is to monitor the status of guest accounts and perhaps participate in the authorization of check cashing and credit terms within policy guidelines.

Other traditional functions within the front office may or may not be the province of a particular individual but nonetheless are performed by front office personnel at some level.

Mail, Messages, and Telephones. Historically, when people travelled by train and boat, hotel stays were much longer than the average stay today. The management of mail in the days before ubiquitous high-quality telecommunications was very important. With the advent of personalized travel by automobile and swift long-distance travel by air, hotel stays became shorter and telephone messages assumed greater importance.

Now, however, with the advent of overnight mail and package service, fax transmission, and sophisticated telephone and voice-mail communication systems, managing mail, document, package, and message service for hotel guests is more important than ever. Today's business traveller relies on modem communications to an extent never before imagined, and a hotel's failure in this context can be costly to both parties. Hotels whose clientele demand high-quality communications service are wise to consider carefully the design and control of the mail, message, and telephone function in the front office.

Guest Service. The bell staff, door greeters, garage and parking attendants, and other uniformed service staff are now seen by most hotel companies as an integral part of the whole service delivery system as opposed to the personal fiefdom of the old-style bell captain. Guest service may also include the specialized duties performed by the concierge. Supervision of these services may or may not be the responsibility of the FOM, but since these personnel participate in many crucial guest service activities, they are increasingly likely to be. Consider, for example, the following processes: initiating the guests' experience (door staff, garage, parking); assisting the guest in transition to the front desk (bell staff); participation in the rooming process (bell staff, luggage); and answering special questions or making extraordinary arrangements (concierge). As these examples attest, guest service is now much more than simply carrying suitcases, and as such should be treated as a professional mid integral part of a hotel's service design. This brief inventory of guest service processes can be compared and contrasted with the "guest service cycle" discussed in Bardi's article to gain further insights about the interrelationships and complexities in the modern hotel front office.

The electrifying job of the front office manager

Students of hotel management are often intrigued by the exciting atmosphere of a hotel lobby. People from all walks of life and corners of the world cross paths to discuss and share ideas, greet family and friends to celebrate speciai occasions, attend conferences to debate issues, or discuss business deals.

Questions concerning arrivals, meeting times, rates, food and beverage services, directions, transportation services, or whereabouts of the management staff and guests create a commotion that seems overwhelming at times. Is there someone in charge here? The preprofessional who sets a career objective as the general manager of a hotel and hopes the required tenure as a front office manager (FOM) proceeds with haste will find the role challenging. If you begin your career in hotel management as a front desk clerk, bell-person, or cashier you have a vast opportunity to explore just who is in charge.

In a 1985 study, Rutherford discussed the important dimensions of the FOM's job, which included communications, facilitation, and organizational interface and technical minutiae Selected job functions reported in the research findings included communications—with guests and employees; facilitating—medical emergencies, selling up, power failure procedures, walking guests due to overbooking, and design of computer system for front office; and organizational interface—with director of marketing, controller, food and beverage manager, and catering manager.

These job skills and interactions require a person to prioritize and to resolve many issues, to make quick decisions based upon sound corporate management concepts, to empower employees, and to refine communication techniques that are exemplary.

Bardi stated, "The front office manager must take an active role in gathering information of interest to guests and in developing procedures for the front office to use in disbursing this information."

This information is also needed by various departments to assist in delivering and organizing hospitality. This is a tall order for the FOM to accomplish, especially considering the total realm of potential information guests may require and from what departments.

Thus the FOM must embrace the charge of becoming a proactive communicator and facilitator. This hotel executive must analyse and seek out what pieces of information the guest will probably need and which departments will need to interact to fulfil these needs. Further inquiry into the role of the FOM can be accomplished by reviewing the elements of a job analysis of this position. Bardi presents a job analysis of an FOM's duties on a typical day.

— Reviews night audit report.

— Reviews incoming reservations for the day.

— Communicates information to employees on all shifts concerning reservations, room assignments, and room inventory.

— Communicates information to other departments-housekeeping, marketing and sales, banquets, food and beverage, plant engineering, and security.

— Resolves guest billing discrepancies and other complaints.

— Prepares budget with general manager and controller.

— Prepares forecasting sheet.

— Conducts business meetings to promote room sales.

— Assists in checkin, checkout, reservation confirmations, updating reservation system.

— Interviews potential front office employees.

— Communicates with night auditor.

— Maintains front office equipment.

Although this list represents only a few of the many duties performed in any one day in the life of an FOM, it provides the aspiring hospitality professional with an idea of the range of managerial activities. The FOM must stay in control of all activities that affect the delivery of hospitality to the guest—a major function of a hotel's financial success. If delivering hospitality to the guest is a major responsibility of the FOM, what are the components of this subsystem of the hotel operation? How does the front office and subsequently the FOM fit in? An answer to this question can be derived from reviewing the "guest service cycle" in a hotel. If the FOM analyses the various guest-departmental contacts, it is possible to gain insights toward understanding how the front office fits in to the efficient delivery of the hotel's hospitality services. The potential guest-departmental contacts in the cycle are:

— *Marketing:* Preparing and administering customer surveys with concern for guest satisfaction, advertising methods, and incentive promotions.

— *Reservations:* Developing and monitoring a reservation system with regard to ease of access to toll-free numbers, fax, national reservation system, and telephone manner of personnel as it relates to reservations, cancellations, accommodation availability, complimentary services and products, and general information.

— *Registration:* Developing and monitoring a registration system with regard to concern for managing a guest transportation shuttle system, ensuring a first-contact greeting, providing assistance with luggage, organizing an efficient checkin procedure, maintaining a room status system, processing credit cards, operating a guest information system that centralizes all communication between the guest and the hotel with regard to housekeeping, food and beverage, maintenance, and other hotel departments.

— *Guest stay:* Coordinating guest communications with all departments in the hotel to ensure guest satisfaction in restaurants, lounges, room service, gift shops, housekeeping services, security, wakeup calls, telephone system, and guest folio availability.

— *Checkout:* Developing and providing an efficient checkout system with regard to coordinating flexible checkout times, providing assistance with luggage, maintaining in-room video checkout option, monitoring guest wait-time in line, and providing folio accuracy and printout.

This listing of components in a guest service cycle suggests the vast array of duties the FOM will encounter in managing the delivery of hospitality services. However, there is one piece of "electrifying magic" that is still required to make front office hospitality relevant to modern service delivery realities: employee empowerment.

Sternberg discusses the concept of empowerment as a granting of authority to employees to make everyday decisions within guidelines. For example, many guests of a hotel feel they are in the middle of a bureaucracy when they want to have a charge adjusted on their account folio. "Step aside and I'll call my supervisor" is too often the response to a guests inquiry of a charge adjustment. After all, cashiers are only doing what they were trained to do. However, the guests don't care what the training was; they just know the system isn't user friendly. As Sternberg emphasizes, if guidelines are established and communicated, cashiers should know what to do. Here is the manager's chance to provide that first electrifying "jolt" of empowerment.

Debated charges within a specified dollar amount can be credited or adjusted without the supervisor's approval. A corresponding control system can be implemented that will reveal the extent of the credit granted per cashier. Another example of providing empowerment opportunities for front office staff is provided by Allin and Halpine in describing quality assurance training at the Waldorf-Astoria:

> While there can be many reasons to combine the positions of registration clerk and cashier, and many aspects were considered at the Waldorf-Astoria, the decision was driven by a desire to improve guest service where its impact is most obvious—at the front desk. Cross-trained employees speed the check-in and check-out process by performing both functions, as the traffic at the desk dictates. Registration clerks can cash checks and cashiers can issue duplicate room keys, in many cases eliminating the necessity of having the guest wait in two lines.

Other opportunities to provide employee empowerment can be identified through careful analysis by the FOM of the progress of the guest through the guest service cycle.

The potential opportunities to serve or misserve the guest can be appreciated when viewed in the context of guests times service contacts. If 12 million guests pass through a hotel company's entire system in a year and each has an average of 12 contacts with hotel staff—guest service staff, housekeepers, front office clerks, and others—that's 144 million chances for the chain to give a good or bad impression.

As the gatekeeper of many if not most of these potential contacts, the FOM is in a unique position to help his or her staff enhance the guest experience. Empowerment is another powerful tool in the FOM's managerial arsenal. The role of the FOM is one that demands a mastery of communication, operational details, and, increasingly, empowerment. The challenging and attractive nature of this role allows the new hospitality professional to try various ways to apply interpersonal skills that will provide a profit for the hotel. It is a challenge that will last a lifetime.

Checking the INs and OUTs of the front office

The purpose of this article is to present both past and current research on the front office employee as well as to apply some general research to the same topic. It is also meant to stimulate some thought when considering this segment of the hospitality industry as a chosen career. The article further identifies the scope of the front office job, what seems to attract employees to it, the problems they face, and how they interact with people both internally and externally. The last part of the article briefly evaluates the hotel front office as a career path.

The front office employees

Visualize this cartoon—Two men are waiting for an elevator. One man comments to the other, "I wonder why the employees in this hotel are so mean and surly?"

The second man replies, "I guess they don't want to be mistaken for guests."

The popular press (*USA Today 1993*) is filled with stories, problems, and "most memorable moments" experienced by travellers. Most hotel employees will tell you, if you wait long enough you'll see it all.

A majority of these so-called memorable moments are neither caused nor influenced by the employees but instead are policies of the hotel, such as: room rates, checkin and checkout times, telephone rate structure, number of nonsmoking rooms available, reservation policies, room amenities, security, room service charges, low-wage and low-skilled employees who do not speak English, real accessibility for the disabled, in-room movie selections, and the list goes on.

Unfortunately the employees, especially those in the front office, receive the brunt of the criticisms and are expected by both management and guest to immediately solve all problems to the guest's satisfaction.

The major responsibilities of the front office employees are fairly well defined by their job titles: bell staff, concierge, doorman, desk clerk, cashier, reservationist, telephone operator, night auditor, and of course the front office manager.

The front office employees must possess an array of attributes that include self-motivation, an outgoing personality, an air of confidence, competence in problem solving, an ability to deal with any crisis, physical fitness with great stamina, and most of all, according to Rutherford, skill in the art of communication on many different levels.

Job attractiveness

The hotel front office may be initially attractive to potential employees because of image portrayed on television situation comedies and movies where the clerk has the guest sign registration book, gives them a key, and the becomes personally involved in many interesting situations. Once reality sets in that the job is not like it is in the movies, it still remains attractive for several reasons.

Front office employees are at the center of the action, and because of multiple tasks, time passes swiftly thereby avoiding job boredom. There is a reasonable structural to the work schedule because the front office operates 24 hours a day, and therefore employee with other responsibilities such as family school may swap or overlap the regularly scheduled shifts. Through the concept empowerment front office employees are made to feel important because they are allowed to make meaningful decisions in order to completely ameliorate any guest dissatisfaction.

The pay, benefits, and chance for advancement are also reasonably attractive. In fact, Marriott's Fairfield Inns are attempting to break the cycle of failure on the part of service employees by a series of rewards for their best employees. Fairfield Inns feels that the guest has two major wants: clean rooms and a friendly staff. By using a computer touch-screen guest questionnaire they evaluate employee performance, thereby providing rewards through pay incentives and bonuses.

Marginal employees who are not able to stand this kind of scrutiny make their exit early in their career. Many properties allow employees to adjust room rates by paying bonuses for upselling or allowing them to offer reduced rates on the spot in order to fill the house. A more sophisticated form of rate adjustment may be carried out through a somewhat controversial practice known as yield management.

Front office personnel face a multitude of problems primarily because they are at the center of the action. That is, they receive all guests' requests and complaints while being expected by management to be exemplary in their job performance. Recently there was a letter in the "Dear Abby" column from a desk clerk bemoaning the fact that guests were making too many (It's Not My Job) demands, such as unplugging the toilet, fixing the TV or AC, supplying more towels or a roll away bed, changing a dim light bulb, retrieving keys from a locked car, and so forth. Apparently this desk clerk did not have a very good understanding of the job description nor that guests may make many such so-called unreasonable demands of a desk clerk.

There is no question that providing service is a complex concept. This may be especially true for front office employees. Some of the factors that may contribute to front office service complexity include:

1. *Autonomy*: The extent to which employees are on their own and must perform without direct supervision of more experienced personnel.
2. *Contact time*: The length and number of times a guest and employee interact, thereby increasing the potential for problems.
3. *Customer knowledge and participation*: The extent to which the guest is expected to reasonably know what to ask for in order for a service to occur.
4. *Team players*: The extent to which other employees may shirk responsibilities, thereby causing the front-line employees undue hardships.
5. *Feedback*: The extent to which employees receive useful and timely feedback from guests or management in order to improve the level of service.

6. *Imprecise standards*: The extent to which employees are prepared to deal with contingencies through known policies and procedures.
7. *Interruptions*: The extent to which a job involves numerous tasks to be performed simultaneously, thereby causing job stress, poor service, and possible burnout.
8. *Repetitiveness*: The extent to which an employee must repeat the same task over and over, resulting in a possible loss of sincerity.
9. *Task significance*: The extent to which a decision may dramatically affect another person's life.
10. *Heterogeneity*: The extent to which both employees and guests are individuals who react unpredictably in dynamic situations.

In addition to the above complexity issues, a struggle for control of the service encounter may also develop between employees and guests. In the case of hotels, the travelling public is becoming more sophisticated and demanding. They possess more knowledge from various media reports.

They acquire knowledge through extensive travelling experiences. The mere fact that the population is "graying" while the service personnel tend to be young generates potential dissonance in service demand and service supply. At the same time, the hotel industry is attempting to become less labour intensive through automation and organizational downsizing, which in itself tends to diminish personal service to the guest.

There is also the issue of satisfaction both on the part of the guest and on the part of the employee. It is obvious that in extreme cases of dissatisfaction the guest will not return nor will the employee perform at an expected high level.

Internal interactions

There has been considerable research concerning comparisons between both individuals and groups, which has led to theories concerning equity and referent comparisons. It therefore comes as no surprise that different departmental employees do not consider themselves equal to others and for that matter probably neither does management. All members of the animal kingdom have a pecking order within and among groups that carries over to the job. The pecking order in the front office may stem from:

— Education level

— Advanced knowledge

— Pay scale

— Mode of dress

— Front of the house versus back of the house customer interaction

— Gender-specific jobs

— Cultural diversity and language ability

— Chance for advancement

— Longevity of employment

— Age of employees

— Servitude level expectation

— Self-motivation perceptions

Education level

The education level of employees is important in the establishment of a pecking order. At first glance it would seem that the more education a person has acquired, the more prestige that person is able to command from peers. This may be true in some cases but not in all. A person could have too much education for the job and therefore lose respect because he or she is thought to be underemployed. A person with fewer years of education may command respect from someone with more advanced degrees, particularly if the training is in a speciality area such as computer technology. There are other equity factors in addition to the number of years of education.

For example, when degree levels are the same, then the subject majored in becomes important, and when the majors are the same the institution becomes important, and so on. Hovering over and possibly driving this entire concept is the educational background of management personnel. This creates a culture that will differ from property to property.

Advanced knowledge

Certain employees are privy to advanced knowledge. That is, they know what is going on before others do. As a consequence other employees must depend on them for information, thus giving them considerable prestige within the organization. This information might be as trivial as a desk clerk or cashier knowing when a guest checks out, which in turn requires other employees such as housekeepers or maintenance personnel to contact them or be contacted that a room is available for cleaning or repairs.

On the other end of the spectrum, power through superior knowledge is nontrivial when an employee has a special skill no one else possesses, such as being able to operate all the computers and master all the software.

Pay scale

The level of compensation is important in the pecking order. It is obvious that minimum-wage personnel are on the lowest rung of the ladder. When tips are introduced there is a mixed status. Since the wages of most tipped employees are tied to the whim and generosity of the guest, their wages may or may not be more than those of nontipped employees. Therefore even though at times they may "take home" more money, the prestige of the nontipped job probably stems from the consistency of wages not the amount. The potential for merit raises also enhances the status of the job. Employees who will seldom advance above the minimum wage generally have no prestige.

Mode of dress

The more formal someone is attired, the more respect they tend to command. A jacket and tie or its equivalent tend to project respect and authority. Someone dressed in such a manner is unlikely to be performing tasks that will get their hands dirty.

Uniforms, on the other hand, present an interesting influence on the concept of pecking order. First and foremost, uniforms are used to identify hotel employees to the guest. Uniforms also tend to promote equalization within the members of a group who are all dressed the same. However, they also perpetuate a class system by guests and between groups, since the uniforms may identify their wearers as having less prestigious jobs.

Front versus back

The front of the house employees, those who come into direct and constant contact with the guest, have an edge over the back of the house employees in job prestige because they were selected to interact with guests. Most front office employees do come into contact with guests but the departments with which they closely interact such as housekeeping and maintenance do not regularly have the sorts of contacts enjoyed by front office staff.

Gender

It is difficult to say whether or not gender in itself represents an element of the pecking order in the front office. Many properties tend to favour female employees as desk clerks because they are better able to diffuse confrontational situations with male guests. Also, there has been a greater acceptance of female employees in the hospitality industry over the past decade. If spite of industry sensitivities to women's rights issues, men still hold the higher-level positions.

In addition, there exists the so-called glass ceiling in which there is an invisible barrier to female managerial advancement. Probably the best reason for such discrimination is the short time that females have been in management tracks. This has resulted in the fact that the position of general manager is still predominantly a male domain.

Cultural diversity and language

It is generally accepted that the trend in the composition of the labour force is toward the infusion of greater numbers of ethnic groups. Ethnocentric feelings of superiority are difficult to overcome. They start with language barriers and continue through cultural differences and stereotyping groups of people into various task performances with little chance for advancement or movement to other departments.

Advancement

Some jobs in a hotel are perceived as stepping-stones to advancement while others are considered dead ends. Many of the top managers of large hotel chains began their careers in the front office, which seems to provide an edge over other departments such as food and beverage. Many of our University of South Carolina alumni tell us that the pathway from food and beverage, housekeeping, and maintenance to general manager is less clear than from the front office.

Longevity and age

The longer one spends at a property or a position, the more respect they command from peers. The term "experience counts" is manifest in senior employees. Not only are they called upon to mentor newer employees, they are perceived to possess inside information, and they generally have the trust and respect of their superiors. The age of the individual does not necessarily command respect. Someone who is considered young and inexperienced may lack the same level of respect as one who is deemed old and possibly should have been encouraged to move on long ago.

Servitude

The difference between service and servitude is not always clear. We are in the service business, but for the most part do not consider ourselves servants. If one is considered in a position of servitude by pests, family, friends, or peers, one's dignity and status may be diminished. The hospitality industry appears to be overcoming this problem through the creation of prestigious-sounding job titles and more valuable and fulfilling job content.

Self-motivation

There may be a lot of truth in the old saying, "Employees are paid either twice or half of what they are worth." At the lower end of the scale are the work avoiders, who feel they are underpaid for what is expected of them and therefore compensate themselves by slowing down, working fewer hours, and generally disappearing. They have little commitment to the organization, are generally dissatisfied with their jobs, and have higher levels of work interference due to child care, family problems, and medical difficulties. On the other end of the scale, we have the overachievers, who pay no attention to the clock. They are highly committed to the organization and seem to derive their satisfaction and compensation from making a difference and completing the task. They are not necessarily workaholics but are individuals who work hard and take pride in what they do, sticking with it until the job is done.

External interactions

Basically a hotel guest wants the following: to have a clean, secure room, to be treated like a guest, and to have all promises kept. If these three expectations are met, the hotel will have a competitive advantage. If they are exceeded, it will ensure repeat business. In the competitive hotel environment of the 1990s a popular current concept is that of *quality*, which is being introduced to operations using the ideas set forth by W. Edwards Deming on Total Quality Management (TQM). In order to accomplish TQM, there needs to be in place a certain organizational culture that accommodates the concept of employee empowerment. Empowerment, of course, allows the employee to make decisions that will, it is hoped, lead to complete guest satisfaction.

This concept has evolved for several reasons. One is that empowerment and TQM have a currently fashionable "everyone is doing it" cache about them. The result is that no one wants to be left out or be deemed guilty of not living up to customer expectations.

A second reason may be a realied need to compensate for the lack of precise service standards, as discussed by Barrington and Olsen. A third reason may be that, due to the cutbacks and overall declines in midmanagement positions, lower-level employees must assume additional responsibilities and accountability.

In order to assume empowerment responsibilities, employees must be trained, monitored, and given feedback, thereby increasing proficiency. There is also an emotional level expected of the employees during the service transaction.

In fact, according to Ashforth and Humphrey, there are three possible levels of emotions: surface acting, deep acting, and genuine emotion. In surface acting, the front office employee puts on a good front by simulating unfelt emotions, such as acting happy through smiling, being respectful, or using the guest's name or addressing him or her as "sir" or "madam."

The employee does this by rote while being careful to give the proper response and expression to both verbal and nonverbal cues. Deep acting is when the desk clerk must really play a role and pretend to be calm even in a stressful situation, such as a fire evacuation. Genuine emotion of course is not acting, but actually feeling the guest's pain. A desk clerk with complete empathy when a guest has been mugged in the parking lot and relieved of all his or her money is a good example of genuine emotion.

Career development

In order to evaluate the career paths of hotel management employees, it is useful to know what initially attracted them to the profession. Based on a survey by Williams and Hunter, the important motivating factors (in order of importance) that helped junior hotel managers to make their career choices include:

— Challenges and satisfaction of the job

— Potential for advancement

— Potential responsibilities and how they are spelled out

— Level of authority
— Fairness of the pay scale
— Amount of guest contact
— Degree that abilities will be used to make decisions rather than perform physical tasks
— Amount of work required
— Number of hours required
— Pay comparisons with managers in other professions
— Amount of paperwork
— Relocation required for job advancement
— Political aspects of the job

Additional factors influencing career success were documented in a recent study by Kavanaugh and Woods. They reported that in order to achieve success on the job, one must possess (in order of importance) the following: communication skills, intelligence, integrity, experience, and a positive attitude. These success factors, although reported differently, tend to corroborate Rutherford's study. A downside aspect of evaluating a career in the hospitality industry involves employee burnout. Although a complex psychological state, burnout is probably the final stage of poor mental health resulting from continued exposure to job stress. According to Vallen's research, there is a strong relationship between burnout and turnover, both of which are very high in the hospitality industry.

Vallen's findings tend to parallel earlier information reported by Barrington and Olsen indicating more than half the front office personnel surveyed felt they were underemployed and not currently in their chosen career and planned to change careers as soon as an opportunity presented itself. An even more interesting statistic revealed that almost three quarters of the front office employees felt they deserved a promotion but saw none in the immediate future. Also in the same study, the high employee turnover rate for the industry was confirmed by the fact that none of the 210 front office employees surveyed had worked in their particular property longer than 16 months.

Complexities of the job discussed earlier as internal interactions could also contribute to job dissatisfaction or burnout. The Barrington and Olsen study provided a further validation of the common job-complexity variables utilized in various job diagnostic surveys, such as being forced to make decisions on the spot, receiving and reacting to extensive feedback from both guests and employers, being expected to possess a variety of skills and talent, and being able to adequately deal with both guests and other employees.

These front office employees were also able to validate a newly created complexity variable, which was the lack of precise standards needed to deal with dynamic situations.

It appears, however, that the imprecise standards variable is being negated somewhat by the empowerment issue, in which the employee is able to deal with situations without fear of violating some obscure or unknown standard. External interactions remain extremely important to understanding the challenges to managing the various complexities of the front office and its employees.

The overbooking

Hotel managers have traditionally accepted the notion that a full house is a gamble. Even the language of the front desk reflects the uncertainty of the reservations system, using such terms as "expected arrivals" and "expected departures." When rooms are scarce, reservations managers gamble on these expectations, using history and instinct to make a rough estimate of how many reservations will be no-shows, how many expected departures will stay beyond their checkout date, and how many unexpected guests, or walk-ins, will arrive seeking accommodation.

All hotels have some kind of policy concerning reservations. The critical profit question is the number of rooms to overbook on a given night. Ideally, the best policy is that which maximizes profit. The actual practice of a specific manager depends on the manager's attitude toward risk.

A risk-averse manager may adopt a very conservative overbooking policy or even undersell to be certain that all reservations can be accommodated.

While conservative overbooking policies avoid the unpleasant prospect of walking a guest, they are likely to result in empty rooms and lost revenue.

The manager who seeks to maximize revenue through liberal overbooking policies runs the risk of walking guests with confirmed reservations and incurring the attendant cost of bad will and possible negative word-of-mouth publicity from those disgruntled guests whose reservations weren't honoured.

The optimum solution would be the development of an accurate forecasting model that would predict room availability and thus indicate the number of reservations to accept for any given arrival date and length of stay. Of the models proposed, some require sophisticated software and costly computer time, while others are too simple to be effective. Therefore, developing an accurate reservations forecasting model may not be the most effective or efficient solution.

An alternative solution is the use of a simulation model to derive an optimal reservations policy. Simulation is an effective technique when used to predict what will happen in a given set of circumstances. It is particularly useful in a dynamic situation, such as a reservations decision, when a reservation for arrival on a given day affects the room inventory for several days. Since the circumstances vary from property to property, simulation models must be based on property-specific data.

A detailed global model is doomed to failure. The simulation must be complex enough to take all factors that substantially affect reservations decisions into account but not so expensive or difficult to use that it cannot be tailored readily to individual properties.

Overbooking models

Overbooking is the most widely used management tactic to minimize financial loss due to cancellations and no-shows. Overbooking techniques originated in the airline industry, but early models made some problematic assumptions. Martin Beckmann's airline model assumed that cancellations and no-shows are both independent of time and occur after all reservations have been accepted.

H. R. Thompson's model of airline reservations was the first in which booking levels were calculated independent of time period. However, this model assumed that once the optimal booking level was attained, additional reservations would not be accepted.

In addition to assumptions that don't reflect the dynamics of the actual reservations situation, airline models don't need provisions for multiple-night stays and single- and double-occupancy rates. Marvin Rothstein applied his Markovian sequential decision model, developed for airlines, to a specific hotel. This model was adapted by Shaul Ladany and applied to establishing room-rental policies. Using historical data to estimate probability distributions for reservations, Fred Williams studied reservations, unscheduled checkouts, and walk-ins. The model formulated an optimum reservations level that minimized the expected cost of overbooking and underbooking for a given number of scheduled checkouts and stayovers on the day being tested.

A simplified approach to overbooking using computer spreadsheet software was proposed by William Corney. The model specified long and short costs (costs associated with vacant rooms and costs related to not honouring a confirmed reservation) as well as no-show probabilities, producing expected costs of alternative overbooking policies.

Simulating reality

Simulation allows managers to study complex, real-world systems that can't be adequately described by other analytical methods. Simulation models describe the operation of a system in terms of individual events. In the case of reservations systems, simulation allows each reservation activity to be studied as a separate event.

The reservations system can be divided into individual components, such as booking, cancelling, no-shows, and walk-ins, each of which can be predicted using probability distributions for that particular component. Interrelationships among the components also are defined by the model. When these components are combined and system data collected, the actual operation of the reservations system can be simulated by the computer and its behaviour studied. By altering a single component, managers can ask "what if " questions study the consequences, and develop alternative strategies.

Developing the model

The first step in simulation is constructing a realistic model by including all relevant components. Next, using historical data from the specific hotel, probability distributions are calculated and the model is exercised through simulation. If the initial model produces promising results, a more detailed model can be formulated using statistically valid probability distributions.

The specific steps of the simulation were: (1) Initializing the model by setting the previous day's occupancy level. The default for the St. Ignatius model was 371, the total number of available rooms. (2) Repeating the simulation for a specified number of days forward (the St. Ignatius model used 30 days). Given the previous day's occupancy, the model generated anticipated departures, early departures, and stayovers. (3) The model generated anticipated arrivals, cancellations on the day of arrival, and no-shows. (4) If rooms were available, the model generated the expected number of walk-ins. (5) From the above data, simulated from the probability distributions and the interactions of the various components of the reservations system, an expected occupancy was obtained. This value was entered as the previous day's occupancy in the next iteration. (6) The final step was to calculate profit or loss. Since the model extends over time, the effect of each day's simulation is carried forward to project what occupancy can be expected on subsequent dates. As more data are received, the simulation can be run again with the changed components.

Refining the model

In the model developed for the St. Ignatius, profit was calculated using the equations shown in the accompanying box. The first equation determines profit when the number of reservations is less than 371 (the total rooms available), and the second, when the number of reservations is greater than 371 and an overbooking situation occurs. Management assumed that the penalty cost of $200 times the number of rooms overbooked would be sufficiently severe to reduce excessive overbooking in the simulation model. Testing indicated that this was not the case, however, since instances of 100 overbooked rooms occurred occasionally when the simulation was run.

Anticipating a revolt by front desk clerks faced with walking guests from as many as 100 overbooked rooms, management suggested assigning a more severe penalty—specifically, the number of rooms overbooked would be raised to the 1.5 power and then multiplied by $200. For example, if the model overbooked one room, the penalty would be 1.5 multiplied by $200, a modest penalty of $300. But if the model overbooked two rooms, the penalty would increase to $600 ($200 multiplied by 2 to the 1.5 power, or 3), and three overbookings would cost the hotel $900. Each subsequent overbooking, then, would cost substantially more than the previous one, and the penalty cost of as few as eight overbookings (at not 8 × $200 but 32 × $300) would make the model "think twice" about overbooking to compensate for possible cancellations and no-shows. This change was incorporated in the refined model and is reflected in the second equation.

Running the model

We ran the simulation for 30 trials of 30 days each. Average profit was calculated for each trial and then averaged over the 30 trials. In the first set of 30-day trials, the profit calculations were generated using the presimulation policy at the St. Ignatius, which allowed no overbooking. The maximum number of occupied rooms could not exceed 371. In this case, the average daily profit was $14,352. Next, the model was altered to allow overbooking but no walking of guests, and we ran repeated simulations to determine the maximum reservations level that could be attained without walking any guests. A policy of overbooking by nine rooms (to 380) achieved the objective of not walking a guest while raising the average daily profit to $14,453.

The final simulation allowed both overbooking and walking guests and was run to determine the maximum average daily profit the hotel could realize, considering the penalty cost for walking guests. This simulation did not take into account management's preference for not walking guests but simply determined the maximum number of rooms management could risk overbooking before the penalty for walking guests began to have an adverse effect on profit.

The optimum reservations level for this more liberal overbooking policy was determined to be 386 rooms, or 15 rooms overbooked. The average daily profit of all 30 runs was $14,474. Wide variations in the averages occurred between the simulation runs because of large standard deviations; no changes were made in the marketing strategies. Although this simulation allowed walking, the penalty minimized the frequency. A guest was walked on only 19 of the 900 days, a rate of 2 percent.

It is clear from the simulation model that the St. Ignatius management's no-overbook policy is too conservative. The hotel can maintain a no-walk policy and improve the annual profit by $101 per day, or $36,865 per year. Comparing this policy to the profit-maximization results, the "cost" of a strict no-overbook policy is $44,530, the yearly difference between an average daily profit of $14,474 and $14,352.

While the additional profit in this case is nominal, the result was significant in the model development.

Predicting cancellations

Analysing the data by day of arrival showed some interesting phenomena: (1) Reservations made on the day of arrival were highly volatile, with a high rate of booking and cancellation on the day of arrival. (2) A high level of volatility—bookings and cancellations—also existed with reservations made one day prior to arrival. There generally was insufficient walk-in traffic to fill cancellations. Moreover, since the reservations policy did not allow overbooking, the hotel was placed in the position of relying on walk-ins to fill rooms left empty due to no-shows and cancellations when regular repeat guests had been refused at an earlier date. Because of these findings, we decided to analyse cancellation data using the *least squares* method to determine whether there was a linear relationship between cancellations. To make this determination, we used all cancellations made prior to a target day to forecast cancellations on the target day.

A weak correlation coefficient of r = 0.70 was obtained from the analysis. The regression equation resulting is: the number of target-day cancellations = 7.8 + [0.766 × (the number of early cancellations)]. Although the correlation of the initial data was not strong, additional data might improve the relationship and allow a more reliable prediction of last-minute cancellations.

The next steps

The initial modelling process required less than 40 hours of programming and about eight hours of data collection. The simulation model becomes more useful as more data are incorporated, so we suggested some techniques that would assist the test hotel's management in improving its ability to capture necessary data.

The results of this investigation indicated that management at the St. Ignatius could improve its occupancy and its profit by accepting more reservations than it currently does. Even if management decided to maintain its conservative stance on walking guests, it would substantially improve occupancy and profit by using the results of the simulation.

The next logical step for the St. Ignatius is to run the simulation simultaneously with the original manual system and compare the decisions made using each model. During this time, management can also determine refinements to capture, locate, and add the necessary data. Simple modifications to the existing reservations system could greatly improve the quality of data available for the simulation model. By modifying the simulation results, the management of the St. Ignatius can change or modify components of the simulation to see the effects of changes in policy. For example, analysis of cancellations by market segment might not only yield better simulation data but also give better information for planning marketing strategies.

Enhancing reservations decisions

The ideal reservations policy is one that maximizes profit, given a set of assumptions and conditions. On the surface, this goal is clear. In practice, however, many variables influence reservations decisions. Developing a policy by trial and error is no longer sufficient in today's competitive environment, and textbook formulas, models developed for other industries, and spreadsheet analysis may not be sufficient to account for the dynamic activity that characterizes the reservations function. The simulation model is a relatively inexpensive means of improving management decision making in the vital area of reservations policies. Use of a simulation model compels management to define and formulate the problem and to articulate such variables as the cost of walking a guest. The simulation requires that management obtain relevant data, find a solution, and test the solution. This kind of in-depth analysis helps managers to understand the complexity of the reservations problem. The simulation model then becomes an important strategic tool, allowing managers to test the impact of policy changes without actually implementing them until the optimum solution for their property emerges.

Discounting in the hotel industry

Three busy executives approach the front desk, check in, receive their room keys, and head for the elevator. On the way up to their rooms, the topic of room rates comes up. As it turns out, Roy is paying $20 more than Jeanne, while Jennifer is paying $18 more than Roy. Yet all three have essentially the same type of room. Those of you familiar with yield management already have figured out that this hotel's yield-management system is in top working order. These three guests—all staying on the same night in similar rooms—have received different rates. You might be thinking that those rates are based on their differing needs and willingness to pay. You might also conclude that something differentiates those guests, something like flexibility in arrival dates or differences in when they booked their reservations.

Your conclusions would be wrong. These three guests booked their reservations on the same day through the same source. What differentiates these guests has nothing to do with supply and demand, their needs, or their willingness to pay. The difference is only their ability to "work the system," their willingness to negotiate with the hotel's staff, and their ability to complain.

The hotel industry's discounting philosophy has uncharitably been described in various industry trade publications as being similar to negotiations in a flea market or on a used-car lot. That comparison may be harsh, but it's not far off the mark. In this article we'll explain how Marriott Corporation has applied a more rational approach to discounting, with advance-purchase requirements.

Yield-management pricing

The concept of controlling discounted inventory has evolved into yield management, which gained prominence when the airlines started using it and is now being used in other industries. Ideal conditions for implementing yield management include:

1. Low variable costs
2. High fixed costs
3. Perishable inventory
4. Variable demand patterns
5. Ability to forecast future demand
6. Ability to segment customers according to their varying needs, behaviour, and willingness to pay

While most of these conditions are straightforward, the last characteristic—segmenting customers—is both the most difficult to achieve and the most important. To maximize revenues, most hotels need to separate customers and charge them different rates based on their different needs and behaviour. It is essential both to segment the customers initially and to *keep them segmented.* That is, not only do hotels need to segment customers, but the hotels also need some way to prevent customers from trading down from one price category to another.

A theoretical demand curve can be drawn for each product or service, showing the tradeoff between price and volume. If only one price were to be offered, we would set that price at the point that maximizes revenue. However, the one-price approach for a perishable product like hotel rooms leaves a substantial amount of unrealized revenue.

Price segmentation

The key to the concept is to have a meaningful segmentation strategy in place (for example, telephone companies' business rates versus weekend discounts) that differentiates customers who are willing and able to pay higher prices from those who are willing to change their behaviour in exchange for a lower price point. The market for hotel rooms is anything but homogeneous. Hotel guests have a wide range of needs. But most hoteliers are well aware that the transient market (that is, nongroup market) can be split into two major components—namely, business travellers and leisure travellers.

Within those two categories are guests displaying a wide range of objectives, but again guests can be grouped according to their buying traits. Any guest's purchase decision will be made upon the particular circumstances of time, place, and purpose of trip. For example, a vacationer at a destination resort may be prestige conscious and quality oriented, but can be flexible about the specific destination and exact timing. By the same token, a business traveller might have to be in a particular place at a particular time, but can be flexible about the exact hotel location.

Taking advantage of those characteristics, recent hotel marketing strategies have attempted to expand the price-elastic market segments (leisure travellers) through innovative rates and packages, while protecting the price-inelastic business revenues from dilution or trade-down. That approach has resulted in increased efforts to segment markets based on the perceived needs of the target market. Until recently, those efforts have been aimed at clearly identifiable groups (for example, AARP, government employees). Such programs, based on the individual's *status*, have been widely accepted and implemented.

In contrast, segmentation practices that employ restrictions based on the booking characteristics of the guest (for example advance purchase) rather than on status or group membership have stirred controversy. The strategy of matching different rates against different purchase behaviour is not new. Airlines have refined the practice with their nonrefundable, advance-purchase, Saturday-stay bookings. Theaters use time of day and a person's age to segment customers. Telephone companies' rates, based on time of day and day of the week, have been in place for many years.

The negotiation problem

What phone companies, airlines, and theaters do not do is negotiate rates individually with their customers. The rules for, say, telephone service are clearly structured and logical. For many hotels, the procedure seems to be one of quoting the highest rate and allowing the customer to talk it down. That strategy has had two outcomes. First, hotels have seen an erosion of their rack-rate and corporate-rate room-nights over the last several years, while the number of discount room sales has increased substantially.

The second outcome is more difficult to document. It is the perceived lack of integrity in a hotel's interactions with its customers. In the case of the telephone conversation that we mentioned, the caller was presented with four different rates. Customers who pay one room rate and later realize they could have negotiated a lower room rate might think ill of a hotel. What emerges is a picture of lodging as the used-car business of the American service industry.

A strategic approach to rate setting

As customers become more sophisticated in manipulating the current pricing system, hotels will eventually be forced to modify their pricing structure. Rather than allow that modification to be made at random, we have been testing a strategic approach to room rate structures. Before we begin our comparison of the three strategies, we should interject that there is a fourth approach: the status quo. That approach is not particularly strategic. Based on the industry's current direction, we don't believe it is viable.

A single rate

The first approach is to offer a single rate for all transient inventory (nongroup, noncontract). That rate can change according to the season or the day of the week. Such an approach is easy to administer and easy to explain to customers. Sophisticated yield-management systems would not be necessary. The one-price strategy, however, fails to respond to peaks and valleys of demand and does not respond to customers' ability or willingness to pay. Some guests will be paying less than they are willing to pay, while others will find the rate too high and go elsewhere, possibly leaving the hotel with rooms it could have filled by using another strategy.

Rates by room type

A second approach is to set rates according to differing room characteristics (for example, size, view, floor level). This approach is currently used by many hotels. It, too, is easy to explain to customers because there may be a perceptible difference in the rooms offered at different rates. It improves on the one-rate approach by allowing the hotel to offer different rates on the same day, thereby realizing more revenue. But setting rates by room type also has several disadvantages.

It certainly wouldn't work for a hotel that comprises just one type of room. Even if it had different kinds of rooms, a hotel would be limited by its actual physical inventory in the number of high-price rooms it could sell, so that potential revenue is limited by product levels and not demand levels. This approach to segmentation won't work in markets where customers are unwilling to pay for upgraded rooms and it is operationally difficult for the front desk clerks and reservations sales agents to manage.

Good fences make good profits

The third approach is to erect "fences"—logical rational rules or restrictions that are designed to allow customers to segment themselves into appropriate rate categories based on their needs behaviour, or willingness to pay. Such fences include advance reservations and nonrefundable advance purchases. Those policies allow for instance, price-sensitive customers to gain lower rate in exchange for reduced flexibility.

On the other hand, traditional full-rate customer can have a room whenever they please. The important aspect of fences is that they allow hotel to sell discount rooms to one segment of customers without allowing higher-rate customers to trade down. Rates with fences are easy to explain to customers, and every rate has a rationale. Using rate-fence system, hotels can use yield management for 100 percent of their inventory, opening up discounts when demand is weak and closing off discounts during strong demand periods.

The downside of rate fences is that they are more difficult to manage than other approaches. Rate fences require sophisticated reservation and yield-management systems. Moreover, a hotel must have regular rates that are correctly positioned for the marketplace. By introducing fences and other rate restrictions, a hotel can penetrate its intended markets as deeply as possible without allowing higher-paying market segments to trade down. The airlines' Saturday-stay requirement is an excellent example of a fence that separates leisure travellers (who are generally willing to stay over) from business travellers.

Fences must be combined with inventory-control procedures to maximize revenues. That requirement goes beyond the yield management currently practiced by many hotels.

While yield management is effective in selling high-rate rooms during periods of strong demand, it has limited effectiveness in preventing a guest who normally pays rack rate from trading down during times of weaker demand, when discount rates are open. Therefore, the inventory control of yield management needs to be combined with the segmentation control of "fences" to maximize revenues.

A study of airline yield management showed why both inventory control and rate restrictions are mandatory for an effective revenue-management program.

When full-fare passengers were asked why they did not purchase a discount fare, 38 percent responded that the discount inventory was unavailable, and 42 percent stated that they could not meet the restrictions. Only a tiny percentage claimed that they would not have traded down without those inhibiting controls.

The Marriott tests

Late in 1990, Marriott began testing fenced rates in the United States and in parts of Europe. The company examined many types of fences that would sort transient customers into segments. For its first tests, Marriott chose to offer rates that had three fences: advance purchase, no refund, and no changes.

Test one

The first test was a holiday promotion in December 1990. One hundred seventy-nine Marriott hotels offered a "holiday" discount rate of $49 that required a nonrefundable purchase 14 days in advance. More than 54,000 room-nights were sold during this traditionally slow period—over 70 percent of them incremental. Of the customers who used advance-purchase accommodations, 11 percent said they would not have taken the trip at all without the discount-rate incentive.

Test two

The next test was a 1991 summer promotion that featured discount rates of up to 60 percent, with both 14- and 21-day advance-purchase requirements. Marriott wanted to see how customers would react to restrictions during the summer vacation months. Customers voted affirmatively with their credit cards. Almost a quarter of a million room-nights were booked, more than twice as many as originally projected. Two thirds of the room-nights sold under these programs represented incremental business.

Test three

During the periods of November 22-December 2, 1991, and December 13, 1991-January 5, 1992, Marriott again ran an advance-purchase promotion, offering rates of $49, $59, and $69, with a 14-day advance-purchase requirement. While the final results were not available at press time, the initial results were promising.

Test four

In the winter months of 1992, Marriott will again test a program with 14- and 21-day advance-purchase requirements. The company's objective with this test is to assess customers' reactions during a more business-oriented travel period than summer or the holidays. In addition, as many as two dozen hotels will try rates with fences different from those of the main program, such as various advance-purchase requirements, advance reservations,, and partial refundability.

Industry reaction

The industry's reactions to Marriott's tests have been mixed and have ranged across the spectrum from positive to negative. Several companies have deemed the test programs as not responsive to customer needs, while others have begun testing their own rate-fence programs. Perhaps the most telling comment appeared in *USA Today*, where correspondent Doug Carroll wrote: "Hotels also need sophisticated computer systems to manage their sales and keep them from selling too many rooms at low rates." Carroll went on to quote Robert McGrail, executive vice president of Hospitality Franchise Systems, which franchises Howard Johnson and Ramada: "A lot of companies can't handle it." Clearly, the ability of a hotel's reservation system to handle fenced rates will influence management's decision to offer them.

Customer reaction

The test programs featuring nonrefundable rates have not caused the customer complaints that many in the industry predicted would arise. In fact, by implementing a structured, rational set of rules that define discount rates, Marriott is actually making it easier for customers to understand the lodging-purchase process. Market research conducted after the first two tests found that two thirds of those surveyed found the advance-purchase restrictions to be "reasonable" or "fair." Of those who took the advance-purchase option, 87 percent said that they would be likely to take advantage of the offer again. The research also found that 87 percent of the travellers using the advance-purchase program were leisure travellers. Based on its initial tests and market research, Marriott believes rate-fence pricing is the right direction for at least a portion of its discounted rates. The fences served their purpose, as follows: (1) they separated business travellers from leisure travellers; (2) they were easily understood and accepted; and (3) they "grew the market" by attracting customers who otherwise would not have stayed with Marriott or, in some cases, wouldn't even have travelled.

Fencing issues

The idea of fenced rates raises issues regarding ethics, difficulty in administration, reaction from business travellers, and complaints from customers over nonrefundability. In this section we will discuss those issues.

Ethics

Many hoteliers are uncomfortable with the thought of charging different guests different prices based on those factors. The issue hinges on setting expectations and educating customers. In segmenting the market, hotels create different products with different prices. Even if the physical attributes are the same, the last room in the house sold the night of arrival is not the same product as a room booked into a half-full house 30 days before arrival.

Through market segmentation, the hotel is able to satisfy at least two diverse groups. For the leisure guest, deeply discounted rooms are available if they are booked far in advance. For business guests, last-minute rooms are available on demand at a higher price.

Hoteliers seem to be at ease in charging different rates based on an individual's *status*, as shown by the plethora of special rates for such diverse organizations as AARP, government employees, and travel agents.

The differing rates generally have nothing to do with the quality of the accommodations or the cost of services rendered. They are based solely on expectations of customers' price elasticities. Most guests, however, have little control over their status when they make a hotel reservation. We think it is more equitable to have a rate structure based on factors that the guest *can* control (for example, arrival and departure patterns).

Such restrictions as nonrefundable rates clearly represent a shifting of risk (that is, for no-shows), for which the hotel is willing to compensate the guest through a discount. Hotels face a substantial opportunity cost for rooms that remain unsold or are cancelled. If the guest is willing to assume the risk of an empty room by purchasing a nonrefundable stay, the product is different from a room that can be cancelled. The hotel rewards this behaviour with a reduced rate.

Business versus leisure

Some hoteliers might observe that business travellers are tired of "subsidizing" leisure travellers. That perception stems from the observation that business rates are generally higher than leisure rates. Any room rate that exceeds the low variable cost of occupying a room contributes toward covering fixed costs. Because the hotel has high fixed costs, additional room-nights of any kind (at almost any rate) generally help increase profitability. Therefore, additional revenue generated from discounted leisure travel helps limit room-rate increases.

Administration

Advance-purchase rates may also require additional staff to process and keep track of deposits. While it is true that fenced rates may require additional resources, that cost is quickly outweighed by additional revenue that can be gained from targeted discount offers and preventing trade-down.

Customer complaints

Customer service is clearly an issue with fenced rates, especially when customers cannot meet restrictions or change their plans after purchasing a room. We believe that customer service issues are actually less troublesome with fenced rates than those encountered with the unstructured system common today.

While fenced rates are not easy to manage, they certainly can be explained to the customer by reservations sales agents. Unlike the negotiation system, the hotel loses nothing by explaining the rules to prospective guests. The choice is always up to the customers, depending on whether they can live with the restrictions. Simply having a rational rate structure diffuses many of the customer issues hotels face today.

Hotel reservations

Reservations are the lifeblood of any hotel operation. Their value is clear both to guests who know they will have a place to stay and to hoteliers who know they will have their rooms filled. The reservations process is so commonplace that hoteliers and guests alike rarely give it a thought—until something goes wrong. In this article, we will argue that a reservation even a telephone reservation, is a contract. Moreover, a small study we conducted indicates that most hoteliers seem to recognize this fact. Suppose someone writes an inn requesting that it reserve a room for him on a certain day. The inn writes back, agreeing to make a reservation. Now say that the party arrives on the agreed-upon date but is refused a room. Has the inn violated a contract with the prospective guest, and can that person sue? Say instead that the guest never arrived, leaving the innkeeper with an empty room during the high season. Can the inn successfully sue the guest?

There seems to be some division among legal authorities on this question John E. H. Sherry, of the Cornell University School of Hotel Administration, argues that the reservation is not a contract unless it is confirmed—meaning that either payment has been made in advance by the guest or that payment is guaranteed by some responsible third party, such as a travel agency or credit-card company.

In his volume on hospitality law, Sherry states: "a reservation will be treated as a contract when there can be found an offer and an acceptance." This is undoubtedly a correct statement of the law, but then he adds: "The necessary consideration is supplied by the guest's confirmation of the reservation in compliance with the hotel's policy (e.g., by payment of a deposit)."

Sherry seems to be saying that consideration, which is a requirement of every contract, is present only when a reservation is somehow guaranteed. We view this as an incorrect statement of the law, and most legal authorities apparently agree with our position. The mutual promise of an offer and an acceptance is adequate consideration to support practically any type of contract.

Unless there is some explicit reason that this would not be true of a contract to reserve a room, we must assume that a room reservation is a contract. If we offer to buy your horse for $400 and you agree to sell at that price with no further stipulations, we have a contract. No transfer of funds is needed to make the agreement binding. By the same token, if we offer to rent you a room for $40 and you agree to take the room at that price, we have a contract.

Sherry's statement requires further comment. When he says, "consideration is supplied by the guest's confirmation of the reservation in compliance with the hotel's policy," the statement may be true as far as it goes. If the hotel *requires* a deposit before it will grant a reservation, the hotel has not accepted the simple offer of renting a room.

Instead, it has made a counteroffer. The guest must accept the new requirement of a deposit, and only when he does so does a contract result. But confirmation is not necessarily a part of all contracts. In summary, any reservation where there is an offer and an acceptance will create a contract. The consideration is supplied by the exchange of promises not necessarily by a deposit or other confirmation.

Other legal authorities state that a contract results from a simple agreement to make a reservation. In his law text, John R. Goodwin analyses the requirements of a contract and the process of making a reservation and concludes that a contract results from an unconfirmed reservation. Norman G. Cournoyer and Anthony C. Marshall arrive at a similar conclusion in their law text, stating specifically that an oral contract for reservations is valid. Jack P. Jeffries spells out the argument in detail:

When a hotel and a person seeking to become a guest enter into an agreement wherein the hotel is to reserve a room for a definite period of time at a specified price, if either the hotel or the prospective guest breach this agreement, that party may become liable to the other party for damages. This is general contract law. The agreement may be oral or may be embodied in telegrams or correspondence between the parties.

The quote from Jeffries introduces another aspect of contracts that should be discussed—namely, the status of oral reservations (typically, over the telephone). Most forms of contract may be oral; certain types must be in writing to be valid. Contracts between an innkeeper and guest are not among the contracts that must be written. Oral contracts suffer from the defect that they are often difficult to prove.

Under most circumstances it would be preferable to have the contract in writing. Nonetheless, an oral contract to reserve a room would be enforceable if either the guest or the hotelier could prove it existed. The issue of whether a reservation is a binding contract has been considered by the courts in cases dating back many years. In a 1946 case, *Kellogg v. Commodore Hotel*, the plaintiff alleged two causes of action, one for breach of a written contract for reservations with the hotel and the other for damages to the plaintiff's nerves and depression.

At issue was whether the complaint should be dismissed without being considered by a jury. The court never questioned the validity of the cause of action relating to damages based on breach of contract and included no statement that the reservation was prepaid or otherwise confirmed. Almost the entire opinion addressed the question of whether the second cause of action (regarding nerves and depression) was valid. The court's holding was negative on this count, but the case is nonetheless authority for the proposition that a reservation is a contract.

A decade later, *Thomas v. Pick Hotels Corporation* involved a situation where the plaintiff was a black person who had made a reservation by mail with the defendant hotel, located in Kansas. On meeting the plaintiff in person, the hotel employees refused to honour the reservation. The court's opinion included no indication that the reservation was prepaid or otherwise confirmed. Kansas had a civil rights statute, but the two-year statute of limitations in this law had expired. Instead, the court held that the plaintiff could bring his action based on a breach of contract, which had a three-year statute of limitations that had not expired. This case is a most direct statement that breach of a reservation constitutes breach of a contract. At least three subsequent cases affirm that failing to honour a *confirmed* reservation constitutes a breach of contract, although this point has never been questioned as far as we know. None of these cases state that confirmation is necessary to create a binding contract.

Practical reservations

There have been few cases involving breach of reservation contracts because of the reality of reservations. The innkeeper-guest relationship is one of the few forms of business transaction in which it is usually impractical for either party to sue for breach of contract. If the inn breaks the contract by turning away the guest, probably the guest can find other lodging. Even if he can't, the real loss for the inconvenience would not be large (especially since the courts won't allow the cost of depression). If the guest breaks the contract by not showing up, the innkeeper often could rent the room to another person, thereby eliminating a claim for damages.

Even if the room remains empty, the monetary loss would not be large. Either party might sue in small claims court, except that the walked guest would have to return to the locale of the inn to sue for a small sum or the inn would have to pursue the no-show guest in some far-off city. Rarely would there be enough money involved to warrant hiring legal counsel and bringing suit in a court of record.

The crux

If neither party is likely to have significant losses or bring suit, what difference does it make if a reservation is a contract? Is the reservations-contract question completely academic? The answer is that there are circumstances under which the inn could face serious damages. Although cases of this nature have not appeared yet, there has been an increasing trend toward accommodating plaintiffs' claims, and it is probable that in the near future we will see a large assessment against an innkeeper who has refused a reservation.

The rule is that the wronged party can sue only for damages that the party breaking the contract could reasonably foresee. Although it is possible that a prospective guest whose reservation is not honoured may incur damages beyond cab fare to the next hotel, the innkeeper usually cannot foresee such damages and the guest could not recover them. But what if the innkeeper is aware of several negative factors.

Suppose it's Superbowl Sunday or graduation weekend in a college town, when every accommodation for miles around is taken. The rejected guest would have no alternative but to sleep in his car or on a park bench. Should something bad happen as a result—a mugging, a vagrancy arrest—a finding of liability against an inn for all resulting damages is well within the realm of possibility, and such damages would not be small.

Room blocks

The other form of hotel-guest contract, which involves long-term blocking of hotel rooms on behalf of a group or association convention, a] so rarely involves prepayment. These reservations involve large amounts of money. If there is a dispute, the suits, countersuits, and subsequent appeals can be expensive, stretching on for years. The most notable of these cases were discussed in an article by McConnell.

The obvious implication of what has been said above is that reservations, whether confirmed or unconfirmed, should be honoured if at all possible. Of course, the usual reason for not honouring reservations is that the inn is overbooked. Because overbooking is merely a good-faith attempt to minimize the revenue loss from no-shows, your strategy should be to reduce the incidence of no-shows.

Stipulations

Many U.S. inns have developed a number of different techniques for encouraging guests to honour their reservations, using various forms of confirmed reservations and other stipulations. Only a few major inns require a confirmed reservation before 4:00 PM. To pinpoint the types of arrangement most frequently used to minimize the losses from no-shows, we conducted a survey of some 70 hoteliers.

Reservation policies

We asked our respondents to report their policy in three basic areas: (1) *reservation acceptance*—under what conditions do they accept a reservation; (2) *collections and recourse*—what action does the hotel take if a guest fails to honour a reservation; and (3) *overbooked houses*—what is the hotel's policy regarding nonaccommodation of guests.

It seems clear that the practices of most hoteliers correspond to the legal theory that a contract results from an offer and an acceptance. Virtually all the hotels will accept reservations upon receipt of a telephone call, and all would also accept a reservation that arrived in written or telexed form. Ten would not honour a request by a travel agent or a hotel representative without a deposit. (This finding might be another avenue for research.) It seems clear from the data in this section of the survey that hotels are comfortable in accepting reservations in whatever form the request is made—with or without a guarantee, cash advance, or credit-card number. It seems equally clear that contracts between the innkeeper and the guest need not be written for the offer and acceptance to be a legally binding agreement.

Conditions

The conditions under which hotels accept a reservation vary with the operations. The following were typical situations where the hotel would accept the reservation without a guarantee:

— If rooms are available.,

— We will hold only until 6:00 PM.

— Depends on the season.

— If we know the client.

Another typical response was that a deposit or a guarantee must accompany travel agent requests.

Hotels have been timid about pursuing bad debts and dishonoured contracts. While there has been much progress in tightening up controls in this area in the past 20 years or so, hotels still can do little more than write a letter requesting payment (reported by 43 hotels). If they have a credit-card number or corporate account, 66 of the respondents said they would charge that account for the no-show. The survey responses show the difficulty of suing for breach of contract. Just two of the responding hotels would even consider such an action, and nine would use the normal business expedient of turning the account over to a collection agency. We wonder whether the hospitality legacy makes it difficult for a hotelier to do such a rude thing as to turn an account over for collection or whether it's not worth the effort to pursue a lost sale.

Similarly, the vast majority of respondents (50) seemed reluctant to blacklist a guest who fails to honour a reservation by blocking that individual in the hotel's reservation system. Several respondents commented that it depends on how often the no-show occurs, whether the reservation is trackable, or whether there is a recurring problem with a company or individual. In the same vein, a much smaller group of respondents had designed other systems or procedures to enhance collections or control risk exposure in the case of no-shows. The following typical procedures were reported:

— Phone call the day after a no-show.

— Adjust the billing cycle after 60 to 90 days.

— Charge to group master account, if applicable or available.

Walking a guest is anathema to every hotel manager, but it is something each of you lives with on a daily basis when you are fortunate enough to be running at or near a full house. It is not surprising that, taking a cue from your travel partners in the airline industry (who face overbooking penalties from the Federal Aviation Administration), hotels now offer the walked guest a number of negotiating points and offers.

Most of the hotels in our sample will pay for a guest room and transportation to a similar hotel, and the vast majority will contact the guest with a formal letter of apology. In most instances, some combination of these procedures will be sufficient to prevent the guest from seeking legal recourse.

Most sophisticated travellers understand that hotels' problems in managing customer demand are similar to those of the airlines. Most hotels, on the other hand, employ a hierarchy of desirability regarding which guests may eventually be walked. Under most circumstances, members of frequent-traveller programs, regular corporate guests, association officers, and meeting planners are seldom among those walked.

Practice meets theory

There is a close convergence between the theoretical aspects of contract law and the actual practice employed by hotels. Oral contracts are binding according to the theory of contract law. In practice, they are employed extensively by most hotels. Confirmed reservations (in the sense of prepayment) are not necessary to create a binding contract to rent a room. In practice, confirmation is only one of several arrangements employed by major hotels. Only when a large number of rooms (and, hence, a large amount of money) is involved are legal procedures important.

American concierges set service standards

Two things seem apparent regarding the concierge in American hotels. First, concierge service has become part of the definition of the hotel product for upscale properties. Second, guest-oriented service standards set by concierges have transcended the hotel industry to be embraced by other businesses.

Expanding concept

At the same time, the philosophy of the concierge has been adopted as the guiding principle of service for entire hotel operations. "Every mission statement for every major hotel chain contains the words or idea of exceeding guests' expectations," Silverman said. Not only that, but the concept of the concierge has expanded beyond the hotel industry. Stiel pointed out that other businesses are installing the concept of the concierge into their own operations. Such enterprises as retirement communities, office buildings, and department stores now have persons designated as concierges. "Each one has its own twist, but the basic concept is to put service up front and make it noticeable. It's a point of difference and it's so visible," Stiel said. She was consulted by such firms as Nordstrom and the Trump Shuttle when they installed their concierge desks.

PepsiCo has developed an unusual adaptation of the concierge in its Purchase, New York, offices. Noting that employees were frustrated by not being able to take care of personal errands (or that they were taking work time for personal matters), the company developed a concierge service that has been wildly popular with employees—so popular that it will eventually be marketed to other corporations (under the name Xtra Ours). Corporate concierge Andy King is probably the first concierge with that title.

Management connection

While a franchise corporate concierge is noteworthy, it may not serve to advance the cause or position of hotel concierges. Their status depends largely on the hotel's management, and not all management teams understand the full ramifications of concierge service. "We still haven't succeeded in gaining general understanding on the part of management of what we do and how we do it so they have more trust in us," said the Inter-Continental's Silverman. "Staffing has to be sufficient. Those nice words about exceeding customer expectations have to have meat behind them. Management must create the environment to make exceeding expectations possible."

The kinds of resources a concierge needs actually involve having the hotel hire a team of concierges, as Stiel sees it. "The concierge is not a person. It's a staff. No one can do this all alone—and who would want to?" she said. In her view, a minimum team would have at least four persons working in pairs who divide the day into two shifts. In addition, three other persons would run errands, and an additional concierge might be responsible for late-evening coverage. In all, Stiel believes, a full staff would be six or seven persons. Neary's Carlyle staff comprises four persons, plus messengers to run errands. His desk is covered from 7.00 AM to 11:00 PM.

Having two persons together at the desk is essential to the provision of full concierge service. "We're busy. It's nonstop. The phone doesn't stop ringing," Neary explained.

"Some managers think it's an easy job, so some concierges are handed the club floor in addition to their regular duties," Stiel said. "But you can't be at the desk for 12 hours trying to fulfil impossible demands and perform perfectly with no assistance and no one to run errands." Silverman pointed to the diminished service resulting from understaffing: "If you have four calls on hold and ten people in front of you, it's hard to exceed guest expectations."

Some hotel manager's do understand the concierge position, however. Neary feels substantial support from the Carlyle's managing director, for instance, and The Worthington provides a traditional, full-service lobby concierge in the traditional mold.

In the estimation of the full-service concierges, only a person who offers the traditional full service should carry the concierge title. Even after more than a decade, some hotel managers hand the concierge title to a person who may be little more than a beverage server. "You don't get a concierge just by pinning on a name tag and hanging up a sign," Stiel said. "In some cases, hotels are contracting with tour companies to take over the so-called concierge desk, even though those companies cannot do what a full-service concierge can do."

Silverman added: "Some managements have what you might call a 'lobby-glamour' syndrome. They hire charming people who are nice to look at. The issue is whether they have the contacts to get guests into sold-out restaurants. We are still arguing for professionalization of the position."

Golden keys

The concierges have done more than argue for professionalization, however. Through their trade association, Les Clefs d'Or, they have created a professional certification program, which includes an examination among its requirements. Even to join Clefs d'Or requires a minimum of five years of hotel experience, including three years behind a hotel concierge desk. The organization retains its focus on the classic hotel concierge. Persons with the concierge title in other businesses, such as apartment buildings, are not considered for Clefs d'Or membership.

Even though the number of hotels with concierges has stabilized, membership in Clefs d'Or has expanded over the past decade from about 50 members in 1983 to over 200 in 1993. The organization's 1993 conference was attended by more than 250 persons, compared to perhaps 30 for its 1983 meeting.

Clefs d'Or has become a mechanism for improving concierges' effectiveness. Through the organization, concierges have built a formal relationship with such service companies as American Express and American Airlines. "American Airlines has special numbers and service agents for concierges only, because our clients are their first-class and business-class customers," Silverman explained. "We can arrange for VIP services around the world and have flyers met at curbside." AmEx publishes an international newsletter in conjunction with concierge service, and Clefs d'Or is in discussions with it to enhance services to gold- and platinum-card holders. Also backed by AmEx, Clefs d'Or has joined in support of the Academy of Travel and Tourism, a private foundation that teaches tourism topics in public schools. Finally, Clefs d'Or has moved beyond issues of professionalism, education, and business relationships to philanthropy, "We have started a foundation to support persons with life-threatening diseases," Stiel said.

Stability

At a time when turnover in hotels is at legendary proportions, concierges remain remarkably loyal. Before Stiel became a consultant and trainer, for instance, she was concierge at the San Francisco Grand Hyatt for 16 years. Silverman left her position at the Hotel Westin Chicago for the Inter-Continental Chicago only because it represented an opportunity to begin at a brand-new hotel. Neary has been at the Carlyle since 1978. The stringent membership requirements for Clefs d'Or and the need to build up a well of information and contacts tend to discourage movement, although some people do move from one hotel to another within the same city. Stiel observed, however, that if a person is resourceful, moving to a new city and learning about it would not be a problem. Occasionally, a hotel or resort will recruit another operation's top concierge.

Silverman believes that the concierge offers more than just an island of stability in a sea of turnover. The concierge may be the one familiar face for repeat guests, in view of the tremendous turnover at the front desk due to promotion and departure. But Silverman offers a suggestion for hotels that cannot afford a full-time concierge or those that have a sharply seasonal business. "Hotels are now hiring many part-time workers. My idea is that Clefs d'Or should prepare for the 'temping of America' by training a group of people to be concierge temps, perhaps using the AH&MA as a clearinghouse. That would be particularly effective for resorts or other seasonal properties," she said. Not all resorts want or need a person with the concierge title, however. For years, the bell captain at the traditional modified-American-plan resort has taken care of guests in much the way that a concierge does.

At the Homestead, in Hot Springs, Virginia, for instance, the bell stand in the lobby has virtually all the information guests need and the bell staff stands ready to take care of guests' wishes of any kind. "It's worked for them for years," Silverman acknowledges. "Some hotels have other titles that really provide the service—and they *do* provide service. The point is to have a designated place where information is organized. Old-line bell captains have the information and the organization, so they are able to do the job."

Concierge consultant

As the first concierge consultant, Holly Stiel has found the educational task to be twofold. "You can teach certain organizational skills to concierges and instruct them in professional attitudes and standards, but you also have to teach managers to understand the role," she said. "Without a good manager, you cannot have a good concierge." The essence of the concierge, however, cannot be taught, according to Stiel. "The basic attitudes must be inherent in the person. She or he has to be a bit of a detective, have the desire to do the job, and want to figure things out," she said. "One thing a concierge often says is 'I don't know,' but that is always followed by 'I'll find out.' The people who are best at this are in the 'giving' professions (e.g., nurse, teacher, social worker)."

Stiel has completed what is probably the first book on how to be a concierge, but the instruction in the book is all by example. "The book is full of concierge anecdotes to show the kind of thinking required to do the job well," she said. "I want to inspire people about the concierge role." The collected anecdotes also make interesting reading. They are similar to the story Neary told of a case he recently handled. "Things that seem easy have a way of turning out to be difficult," he recalled. "One of our guests wanted the videotape of a program he had seen on television the night before, but the guest didn't know which channel or what program—only the topic. First we had to sort through the 50 channels of the New York cable system to figure out which channel it could have been distributed on. It turned out to be the public access channel. Then we had to track down the producer, who was out of town. Eventually we located the producer, who had the only copy of the tape in existence, and we were able to make a copy for the guest."

Concierge tech

Many hotels are applying technology to reduce the labour intensity of guest service, for example, with computer-generated wakeup calls and voice-messaging systems. Far from being a threat, computer-based technology may amplify a concierge's ability to serve guests. For the past few years, individual concierges have used stand-alone desktop computers to maintain their records of information sources. That's a step beyond maintaining guest histories at the front desk, which is also a valuable guest service, but Stiel points out that the personal touch added by the concierge is important.

"We now have computerized concierge files directly connected with the hotel's property-management system, for example, an HIS system," Silverman said. "Instead of separate data bases, the concierge software is now part of the hotel computer system." Silverman expects additional enhancements of the concierge's technical abilities to "move the position into the twenty-first century."

The concierge, like the hotel industry itself, has not achieved the blend of technology and management finesse that is metaphorically referred to as being in the next century. Since that century is a scant few years away, the concierges hope soon to complete their project of educating management to the full scope of their role in the hotel.

Marriage

"Every industry is at a crossroads—entering an age of enormous technical potential. That's true of the hotel industry, as well, especially internationally," Stiel said. "We need to open a dialogue between concierges and their managers. The concierge is the eyes, ears, heart, and soul of the hotel. A properly functioning concierge desk is a 'marriage' between a manager and a chief concierge who has a staff of people who understand the job. So, that's the concept for the next few years: educating managers, especially in America," Stiel continued.

Progress for women

Although the educational job seems large, concierges have made considerable progress in the relatively short time they've been in American hotels. In addition to making the American branch of Clefs d'Or a vital organization and a force for professionalization, one particular achievement of concierges is to demonstrate conclusively how effective women are as concierges.

When American hotels originally hired women as concierges, there was some concern internationally that women could not do the job. Today, women have been accepted internationally as concierges. Silverman herself is third vice president of the international Clefs d'Or and the first woman on the international society's board of directors—positions she believes would not have been given to a woman even ten years ago.

Whether women or men, American concierges have clearly demonstrated the value of the enhanced service they offer guests. That value is shown in the expectations guests have when they stay at upscale hotels. It is shown in the fact that other businesses have adopted the concierge concept for their own. And it is shown even in the resistance many hoteliers have had to cutting back on concierge service, when they at least strive to keep the title and the service in some form, rather than eliminating it entirely.

Middle managers

Call him Jeff Colburn. He's 31 years old and has been working in hotels for nearly ten years. Two years ago he was promoted to reservations manager at the Osborne, a 650-room eastern U.S. property, where he supervises 16 employees. Jeff is typical of the almost 100 hospitality managers from across the country who helped us create a composite picture of the communication activities that shape their work on the job. Through on-site meetings, telephone interviews, focus groups, and questionnaires, they shared their perspectives on the challenges of business communication in the 1990s. In their own words, respondents like Jeff tell us what it's like to be managing in the middle.

A review of participants' responses to some general questions regarding their daily communication will help to determine how you and your colleagues compare to your peers across the country. In this chapter we will explore the challenges middle managers face in facilitating upward communication, in communicating downward to their own work group, and in maintaining effective relationships with other middle managers. We will then present guidelines for increasing effectiveness in what appear to be the critical communication situations hospitality managers face.

Managerial communication

Why is it so important to understand how to communicate effectively? For one thing, no other managerial competence is so directly tied to job success. Every one of your daily activities—motivating, influencing, explaining, delegating, coaching—depends upon communication effectiveness.

In fact, you probably spend over 80 percent of your day communicating. Just think what a difference it would make if you improved your performance by even 10 percent! As the workforce becomes more diverse, communication skills will be even more important in determining the ease with which all employees respond both to their co-workers and to their daily job requirements. In your leadership role, your communication behaviour provides a model for your employees and influences morale, organizational climate, and, ultimately, both service quality and productivity.

One of the first steps toward improving communication on the job is to attain a better understanding of what goes on during the course of a typical day. It's easy to make assumptions about how someone like Jeff spends his time behind the scenes at the Osborne. You can guess whom he interacts with and how satisfied he is with the way he handles these regular encounters. It would be more helpful, however, to ask him questions that would create a vivid and accurate picture of his communication activities.

A communication profile

Several questions appear to be particularly important. First, to whom are middle managers talking? When this group was surveyed, every respondent indicated that he or she communicates with subordinates several times each day. Over 90 percent of those surveyed also talk daily with their colleagues. Relatively less time, however, is spent in face-to-face interaction with supervisors and guests; 22 percent of the managers surveyed said they talked to their supervisor only once a week. Over 30 percent talk with guests less than once a week.

Second, how difficult do managers think it is to communicate with these various groups? Employees, they say, have more trouble expressing ideas to their manager than managers do in communicating with employees. Sixty-one percent of those surveyed felt that employees experienced significant or great difficulty communicating upward, while just under 50 percent felt managers had significant problems communicating down to their subordinates. In contrast, 70 percent of the respondents found very little or no difficulty expressing ideas to their colleagues.

It may be helpful also to look at the *types* of communication that take place, and how much skill managers believe they have in performing each task. As you might expect, managers are slightly more likely to send a memo to their supervisor than to their employees. Written communication, however, usually takes the form of a report or business letter.

On a scale of one (seldom) to six (frequently), 63 percent of the managers surveyed indicated that they frequently wrote reports, and an even greater number said that they frequently wrote business letters.

Middle managers also appear to spend a good deal of their time engaged in oral communication activities. Over 30 percent of those surveyed frequently deliver formal presentations (only 15 percent said they seldom stand and speak in front of a group), while 35 percent participate frequently in some form of interviewing. The highest categories, however, were resolving conflict and providing feedback. While 60 percent of the responding managers indicated that they frequently provided feedback to their employees, 72 percent of our sample frequently find themselves resolving conflicts.

Mixed messages

Now we know that managers spend a lot of time engaged in written and oral communication activities. The next question is, how skilled are they at each of these tasks? To answer this question, the managers were asked how well they felt other department heads and supervisors handled each type of communication situation. Using the six-point scale mentioned earlier, not one manager gave a rating of six to his or her colleagues on *any* task! While the managers felt their peers handled memos moderately well, 34 percent of those responding indicated that their peers wrote poor business letters, and about the same number gave them low marks on report writing.

Writing was not the only skill managers felt their peers lacked. The most troublesome area of all was delivering formal presentations. Over 65 percent of the respondents gave the category "making presentations" a ranking of three or lower and over 40 percent described their colleagues' presentations as poor. Although managers find themselves providing feedback frequently, 34 percent believe they do it poorly; fewer than 10 percent feel their colleagues do a good job at this task. Managers believed their peers were moderately skilled at both resolving conflicts (84 percent) and interviewing.

This information should given you a general idea of how Jeff spends his time each day, and what his colleagues think about his communication behaviour. Numbers, however, don't tell the whole story. Let's look at some common communication situations, as they affect Jeff's relationships at work and his ability to accomplish his management tasks.

Voices from the trenches

The lines of formal communication are generally discussed in terms of the upward, downward, and horizontal movement of messages. Although we know that informal networks transfer information without regard for level or position, the formal channels are important to recognize and understand because managers can plan and control the nature and frequency of information transmitted in this manner.

Once communication patterns have been determined, these networks can be analysed and communication strategies implemented that will improve organizational effectiveness. First, let's look at the vertical dimension to (1) see what problems Jeff's subordinates have communicating upward to him and (2) examine his communication downward to his work group. Finally, we'll see what happens when he communicates horizontally with other department managers.

Upward communication

As a typical hospitality manager, one of Jeff's most serious problems is getting his employees to share information with him. A frequent complaint is that his employees are reluctant to communicate bad news. They seem afraid of reprisal and often don't explain the real problem, even when he asks them directly.

At the same time, Jeff may behave in the same way with his boss. As one manager noted, this pattern is not unique to middle managers and their employees. It occurs in upward communication at all levels. A restaurant manager described the following situation:

> You find out that evening that you messed up—you missed a birthday cake. Do you turn around and talk about it? Do you say anything to the owner when he asks how the night went, when you know it will

> make his blood pressure rise and the veins in his forehead pop out? I mean, you feel caught in the middle. You insulate him from things and your people insulate you from things. This whole thing gets perpetuated.

Why this reluctance to share bad news? Managers were clear about the possible causes of their problems and fears. One explanation was that subordinates at all levels aren't asked often enough for their opinions or ideas. As one manager explained:

> Our GM never asked how things were going. I mean, it just never dawned on her. She knew people were coming and going. Then a year later, we mentioned the turnover statistics and it's like, "Well, yes, hello, hello—where have you been?" By then, imagine the organizational problems that had been caused! She had shut herself off and then it was hard to get back.

The most frequent explanation, however, was that employees fear the consequences of communicating bad news. The following stories are typical:

> My boss is old school. If he didn't want to hear something, if it was a problem, that meant that somebody had to be fired. Now he's slowly begun to change his thinking. It's not that somebody needs to be fired; it's just that somebody needs to be trained a little better.

Another manager told of the following incident:

> I got sick and tired of having the owner go into the dining room and ream out my waiters, which is very embarrassing when you have a roomful of guests. When he got through with the waiters he'd go to the captain and do the same thing. Then, when he got through with the captain, he'd come to see me. The captain ran one dining room; I ran three, So I'd get it three times as long. It's very discouraging; you're trying to do your job, and you have this guy screaming at you.

Encouraging upward communication

How can supervisors encourage subordinates to tell them what's going on? First, it's apparent that Jeff's employees must believe that he will listen openly and objectively to their problems and concerns. If he has a reputation for having a quick temper or for discounting what others sky to him, the flow of information will be cut off. Jeff would be wise to practice his listening skills, by asking questions and checking his perceptions rather than making critical, judgmental statements. The ability to listen to the entire message without becoming emotional is key.

As one manager discovered, intimidated employees often resort to writing, thus blocking open, two-way communication. In one example, a manager described finding a note taped to his office door. It said, "If the problem I told you about yesterday isn't resolved right away, I'm going to quit!"

Jeff also needs to take the initiative and to be creative in his own problem-solving activities. What can he do, within the context of his particular property, to facilitate upward communication? As an example, one of his colleagues described the following plan:

> I'd get everybody in one place at one time and say, "Okay, here's the situation. Take five minutes and read this and then I want feedback." I wouldn't let them leave until I heard something from every single person. "Is this garbage or do you think ifs something useful? If it's garbage, why do you think so?" I had really good results with that approach.

Another organization took this idea even further, scheduling monthly "town meetings" with the general manager herself. Employees were encouraged to raise questions and discuss issues firsthand.

Not only must managers themselves be creative and persistent in their efforts to facilitate upward communication, they must also recognize the impact their daily communication behaviours have on their employees.

Downward communication

Although Jeff would like to think that communication problems occur primarily because of unskilled line employees, communication breakdowns are seldom one-sided. His employees have their share of legitimate complaints about the way he handles information. As a front desk employee explained:

> There's a real problem getting information up to management. We'd sit down in a brainstorming session and say, "Okay, how can we improve operations in terms of giving better quality service to our guests?" We'd come up with the greatest ideas. We'd sit down with the front office manager and talk to him, but nothing ever came back to tell us whether something was being done with our ideas. Were they filtered up, or did they just get lost somewhere along the line? Do suggestions work if you never hear anything back?

As this comment shows, downward communication is critical.

Two of the most serious communication problems, from the perspective of middle managers, are (1) lack of concrete information and (2) reluctance on the part of managers to explain the reasons behind their decisions. With so much emphasis on cultural leadership, vision, and symbolic management, the bottom line still seems to be that clear and concrete information is needed at the right time and in the right place. One middle manager shared the following thoughts:

> A lot of fine-dining restaurants think that the culture is just supposed to catch on, and that management philosophy just floats around. But when you get to dishwashers and busboys and people like that, the philosophy doesn't really matter. It's still, "What do you want me to do right now? I mean, I know you want a clean bathroom, but what is grout?" Then you have to explain, "This is grout. This is the bowl. This is the toilet brush" and so on.

A second source of misunderstanding comes from managers' reluctance to explain the reasons behind their decisions. One manager described a typical example:

> Our GM decided that she didn't want soft drinks around the front office area. In the past, front office clerks and PBX operators could have refreshments at their stations as long as they weren't visible to the guests. The GM felt there was no way to ensure that the drinks would stay out of sight, so she banned them altogether.

The trouble began when the night manager didn't follow the rules and allowed the night operator to have a drink at the work station. When the morning operators discovered this, they argued that it wasn't fair, and that they could also keep their drinks out of sight. The day manager gave in, and there were again sodas in the PBX area. When the front office clerks found out, they brought sodas into their area, too.

The general manager should have told them from the start that visibility wasn't the only reason for the rule and that it was one small part of an overall effort to increase professionalism and to maintain consistency in the guidelines for all staff. Communicating only the "visibility" issue rather than the larger goal made following the rule difficult. Once employees understand why they are asked to do something, a rule is easier to enforce.

Successful communication strategies

If the examples above sound familiar, it's because middle managers everywhere face similar challenges and frustrations. Below are three steps to take in reducing or preventing common communication difficulties, including using horizontal communication to the best advantage.

Step 1: Communicate detailed information as well as the big picture. Jeff can increase his effectiveness by making sure that the information he conveys to his employees is concrete and specific, and that he encourages employee commitment by sharing the rationale behind the rules and policies he asks them to support.

It's easy to make assumptions about what employees know or understand. Such assumptions, however, are dangerous: employees can perform their jobs well only if they know exactly what is expected. As one manager reports:

> My employees say, "Well, I thought someone would bring it to me. I didn't know it was my job to go get it." I hear such excuses all the time and I think, "Why don't you just look around? Everyone else is doing it." But I say, "Why didn't you ask?" And they say, "I didn't know I was supposed to ask. No one told me." It just goes around and around.

Ambiguous instructions and vague job descriptions, such as "deliver high-quality service to all guests," have limited value in an industry where the competitive edge is defined by attention to detail. How do you know when you've been clear? As another manager says, "You know you're doing okay when all of your employees know how to dust the light bulb."

The recent emphasis on participative management recognizes employees' need to be involved in the decision-making process. Part of this philosophy requires that managers explain the reasoning behind their requests. When employees feel left out of the process, they are much less likely to follow rules. The hospitality industry, in particular, depends on employee involvement and independent decision making to a much greater extent than other industries. For this reason, helping them to see the "big picture" has a direct benefit. One manager explains: The people who deliver the service are the lowest paid. In manufacturing, people are working the lines and building the gizmos, but there's somebody there checking those gizmos before they go out of the factory. Our product is how that desk clerk talks to the guest, and a lot of times we're not even there.

Jeff's challenge, then, is to promote a feeling of confidence and commitment among all of his employees. When his staff know exactly what is expected of them and when they understand the larger picture, they can see how their actions contribute to accomplishing the organization's goals.

Step 2: Talk *with other managers—communicate horizontally.* Jeff and his staff know there is a lot they could do to improve interactions with employees. Jeff knows, too, that when he implements some of the ideas he's been considering, his interactions with his staff are almost certain to improve. However, it's the comments from his peers that upset Jeff the most.

While a majority of the misunderstandings he experiences with his employees could be resolved by learning and practicing specific communication skills, his fellow managers report problems of a different nature. It appears that many of the challenges middle managers face when communicating with their peers result from specialized perspectives, defensiveness, and reluctance to share the necessary information. In fact, a significant number of Jeff's colleagues indicated that rivalries, gossip, and back stabbing were not unusual. In addition to personality conflicts, which make working together difficult, there was considerable finger pointing and "cover yourself" tactics, especially in departments that overlapped.

Competition for resources and loyalty to a particular department (rather than to the organization itself) caused many managers to take a myopic view. One manager writes:

> Since hotels are organized with many different specialists (department heads), it is natural for manager to have trouble empathizing and listening to a colleague with a different perspective. It easy to forget that we all have the same overall goal.

This loyalty to a particular department or are frequently creates a situation where manager find it difficult to be open-minded. One manager noted that this problem is particularly appeared during meetings:

> Generally, managers go into a meeting with a predetermined outcome and spend all of their time trying to reach that outcome without listening to considering the others' input.

Managers were also quick to blame others for problems on the job. Often, problems resulted from insufficient information. In many case managers perceived that their colleagues with held information, assuming that "subtle change" in their areas won't affect other department The resounding response, however, was, "B they do!"

Step 3: Foster openness and trust. Jeff feels much less in control of the horizontal communication at the Osborne than he does when communicating upward and downward. Consequently, he feels less able to facilitate positive change. When working within his own department, Jeff has a sense of authority and power. It is relatively easy for Jeff, as the department supervisor, to exert influence on the situation at hand. When communicating horizontally across department boundaries, however, he wonders how one manager can have any significant impact on the behaviour of his or her peers. He feels, too, that at least part of the problem has to do with managers' attitudes and lack of team spirit. Clearly, strategies that may work with a reluctant dishwasher will likely be inappropriate when used to influence the food and beverage manager.

Although the methods he uses with his colleagues may not be as simple and straightforward as those he finds successful with his staff, Jeff's behaviour still has a significant influence on other department managers. A few changes in his own attitudes and communication practices will, over time, affect other managers. He can begin by approaching *all* communication situations with an open mind and by practicing behaviours that are likely to reduce defensiveness in those with whom he communicates. It is difficult to stay open-minded, especially when competing for limited resources or engaging in some other type of persuasive activity. One manager described the situation well:

Manager-to-manager communication is affected by each individual's insecurities. Before we discuss a problem we are having with another manager, we try to remember that there are two sides to every story. Many managers enter into a conversation already defensive and that tends to put the other manager on the defensive as well. Building a supportive climate, characterized by trust and information sharing, takes time. The first step, however, is the recognition that "from the other person's point of view, she's probably right." Remaining open-minded and trying to understand how his colleagues see the situation will enable Jeff to improve communication with his peers. Defensiveness is one of the most serious and frequent managerial communication problems. It can, however, be reduced by practicing the following communication behaviours.

1. Describe the behaviour or problem that bothers you rather than making such judgmental statements as, "That was a stupid thing to say" or "You really blew that sale."
2. Focus on finding solutions to problems, not on placing blame on your co-workers.
3. Qualify opinions and controversial statements with such modifiers as "It seems to me" or "From what I know of this situation" rather than stating your position as if it were the only "right" way to think.
4. Show concern for the other person's position and point of view. Attitudes of indifference, apathy, and superiority may increase feelings of defensiveness in others.

When defensiveness is reduced, trust increases. When the environment is supportive, managers need spend less time protecting their reputation and personal territories and can look instead at the larger picture. When horizontal communication is effective, all managers are facing the same direction and following the same vision.

Teamwork and trust

Perhaps your department managers are not at all like Jeff Colburn. Even so, it might be helpful for them to know some of the things we've discovered about middle managers' communication practices. It may be valuable for them to have a better understanding of the challenges others in their position face as they link line employees to upper-level management and as they span boundaries between their function areas.

Although no two properties are alike, middle managers from across the country share common concerns and face similar problems as they perform their daily tasks. Most of those tasks involve communication, and the quality and nature of their interactions directly affect both productivity and service.

Middle managers hold the key. Those who communicate effectively encourage information sharing and provide clear and sufficient messages to their subordinates. They promote a climate of teamwork and trust through their open-mindedness and supportive communication practices.

As middle managers look to the twenty-first century, they will see offices and function areas equipped with new and more sophisticated hardware. If they look more closely, however, they will notice that only in those properties where information is flowing smoothly through human links is the organization truly healthy and productive.